SWITZER
THE PLAYERS' COACH

BY JIMMIE TRAMEL

TULSA WORLD

SWITZER
THE PLAYERS' COACH

BY JIMMIE TRAMEL

EDITOR
Debbie Jackson

COPY EDITOR
Matt Lardner

DESIGN
Tim Chamberlin
James Royal
Jason Powers

PHOTO EDITOR
Christopher Smith

ARCHIVES
Hilary Pittman

EXECUTIVE EDITOR
Joe Worley

PRESIDENT AND PUBLISHER
Bill Masterson

On preceding page: In 16 seasons as University of Oklahoma head football coach, Barry Switzer amassed 157 victories, 12 conference championships and three national titles.

This page: Barry Switzer is shown at the start of his first season as OU head football coach in 1973.

On facing page: Switzer laughs as he retells a story during an interview at his home in Norman, Okla., in 2012.

Tulsa World Media Co.
315 S. Boulder Ave., Tulsa, OK 74103
First Edition
ISBN: 978-0-692-25450-9
Printed by Walsworth Publishing Co.
Marceline, MO

TABLE OF CONTENTS

PREFACE

Angel or rascal?

Barry Switzer shared a tragic backstory and told the world he was a "Bootlegger's Boy" in a 1990 autobiography.

The continuing story is this:

The bootlegger's boy remains a father figure to legions of former players.

"We are all like little kids vying for your dad's attention," Joe Washington said.

Many former players spend nights at the coach's Norman home like it's the Switzer Marriott. Switzer equipped the house with extra beds.

"To this day, if I come to Oklahoma and I don't call coach Switzer and I don't let him know that I'm here, I'm going to get a call from him," Greg Pruitt said. "He'll say, 'Why didn't you call me? Where are you at? You can't come here and not call me?'... He is mad if you are staying somewhere else."

During interviews for this book, it was suggested to Switzer's former players and assistants that Switzer has an angel on one shoulder and, at least, a rascal on the other shoulder. A chuckle or a smile usually followed.

In separate interviews and without being prodded, people who know Switzer said the coach is sort of like Bill Clinton.

Why? People who don't know Switzer think they have a reason to dislike him. Then they meet him and get charmed. Or they hear perception-altering stories.

Did you hear about Switzer escorting a truckload of furniture to former player Louis Oubre after he lost everything to Hurricane Katrina?

Did you hear about Switzer chipping in to help provide a proper burial for former player Terry Crouch?

Did you hear about Switzer spotting a dog (Stella) in a vehicle on a hot day in 2013 and waiting for the owners to arrive so he could buy her?

The consensus comment from former players on all of the above: That sounds like something Barry would do.

Never mind three national championships at Oklahoma and a Super Bowl victory with the Dallas Cowboys, Switzer's crowning achievement might have been relating to players on a human level and sparking lifelong mutual loyalty.

Washington played nine seasons in the NFL after starring at OU and missed his time with Switzer. Now Washington is the executive director of OU's Varsity "O" Association and cherishes talking with his coach in person or on the phone as often as possible.

Is it fair to say Switzer is the ultimate players' coach? Don't get the wrong idea, warned Washington. He said practices were intense.

"Most people wouldn't think that," he said. "They would think it was easy, lackadaisical, no rules, whatever. But it was far from it. Him being a players' coach, yes, he understood players were important. Players are the most important ingredient of a successful program. And he will be the first to tell you that. I think because he approached it in that particular manner and he obviously put players first, people would say he was probably undisciplined and things like that. I'm sorry. He was disciplined."

And appreciated, still.

– Jimmie Tramel, July 2014

Switzer walks down the sidewalk in front of the first home he built after becoming head coach at OU.

Rivals, never enemies

BY TOM OSBORNE

It was during the sixties, seventies and eighties that the series between Nebraska and Oklahoma truly became a great rivalry. From 1962, Bob Devaney's first year at Nebraska, through 1988, Barry Switzer's final year at Oklahoma, Nebraska and Oklahoma dominated the upper level of the Big Eight Conference. During that 26-year span each team either shared or won outright the conference championship 15 times. Nebraska won two national championships under Bob Devaney and Oklahoma won three national championships under Barry Switzer. Both teams were usually in the hunt for a national championship and were ranked in the top 10 at the end of the season nearly every year. Bob Devaney retired at the end of the 1972 season and chose me to follow him as the next head coach at Nebraska. That same year, Chuck Fairbanks left Oklahoma to coach the New England Patriots and Barry Switzer was chosen to replace him. So, as the rivalry grew, the careers of Barry Switzer and me were inextricably linked.

Unfortunately for me, things did not go well for the next five seasons. We would win nine or 10 games each year, but if we lost to Oklahoma it was not a good season. Our fans would agonize after each loss and the phrase "Sooner magic" began to pop up. It was believed that Barry had our number and somehow Oklahoma would win. After one of those losses, I came home and our daughter, Ann, who was about 7 at the time, informed me that she was going to "move to Oklahoma

Nebraska head football coach Tom Osborne motions to his team during a game in 1997. The Cornhuskers were 13-0 that year and shared the national championship with Michigan. Osborne retired as coach at the end of the 1997 season following an Orange Bowl victory over Tennessee. Nebraska had won two previous national championships, in 1994 and 1995, under Osborne.

since we could never beat them." Years later my wife, Nancy, told me that our three children didn't want to go to school after those losses because of the harassment that they would

As head coaches at Nebraska and Oklahoma, Tom Osborne (left) and Barry Switzer were college football rivals from 1973 until 1988.

receive from classmates. There were many in Nebraska who thought that it would be a good idea to get a different coach. The 17-14 win in 1978 against Billy Sims and a great Oklahoma team helped some, but it wasn't until the early eighties that we were able to win three straight and gain some credibility. Still, the fact that Oklahoma had won three national championships under Barry and we had won none with me as head coach (even though we had come close) did not sit well in Nebraska.

Many people thought that we would grow to hate Oklahoma because of our losses to them and the intensity of the rivalry. This was not the case, as we had great respect for them and came to realize that we couldn't bring Oklahoma down to our level. Rather, we needed to get better, to elevate our level of play from good to elite. We began to recruit quarterbacks who could run. We emphasized the option more because Oklahoma hurt us so badly with it, only we ran it out of the I formation instead of the wishbone. We set aside extra time to work exclusively on defending against the wishbone. The final game in which Barry and I coached against each other, in 1988, we were able to win 7-3 on a cold, wet, miserable day in Norman.

Oklahoma wasn't our enemy, they were our rival and they made us better. We had to change and adjust to play at their level. It took a long time, longer than our fans wanted, but there is no question that being in the same league with Oklahoma and having so much importance attached to that one game made us better coaches, players and a better program.

Most rivalries become heated and sometimes bitter. Although each side wanted to win badly, I never felt that way about the Nebraska-Oklahoma series. There was always a good deal of respect on both sides among players, coaches and fans. I don't recall a single incident in which there was a fight or flagrant foul involving players, or for that matter, nothing major among fans. Very few rivalries can point to that type of record. Both teams had won a lot so there was not a feeling of inferiority, which often leads to ugly behavior. I never taught our players to hate our opponents. We taught respect for our opponents and I think that Barry did the same.

Even though Barry and I are very different in many ways, I believe that the way in which we coached and motivated our players was much the same. We remain good friends to this day and talk frequently. He was kind enough to attend a political fundraiser for me in Nebraska and also attended a retirement party when I stepped down as athletic director. Barry is quite likely more popular in Nebraska than I am, and I have always felt very welcome in Oklahoma. I have done quite a bit of speaking in Oklahoma, often at Fellowship of Christian Athletes events, and have a good relationship with Chuck Bowman, Clendon Thomas, Bill Krisher and J.C. Watts, all former OU players.

The rivalry was never quite the same once the Big 12 was formed. As a member of the South Division, Oklahoma only played Nebraska two of every four years. A rivalry that is not continuous soon ceases to be a true rivalry.

Hopefully things will work out well for all concerned, but most Nebraskans (and Oklahomans I hope) miss the annual game played at a high level each year on a cold Friday afternoon the day after Thanksgiving.

"Oklahoma wasn't our enemy, they were our rival and they made us better. We had to change and adjust to play at their level."

Tom Osborne said the Cornhuskers elevated their level of play from good to elite in order to compete with Oklahoma. He is shown with Barry Switzer at Memorial Stadium in Norman, Okla., in 2000.

CHAPTER 1

Tater Hill

"In his heart, he is drawn to help the people that have been around him and have done things for him and helped make his success."

— Thomas Lott, former OU quarterback

Opposite: Barry Switzer waits with his players before the start of a game against Oklahoma State on Oct. 23, 1982. The players include Paul Ferrer (55), Ricky Bryan (80) and Danny Bradley (1).

TWO-WAY LOYALTY

I t's July 30, 2009, or about 20 years and a month after Barry Switzer stepped down after an absurdly successful 16-year run (12 Big Eight championships, three national titles) as head football coach at the University of Oklahoma.

Switzer, behind the wheel of a Mercedes, is, with the blessing of law enforcement officials, blazing down turnpikes and highways because he wants to be at a memorial service for former OU All-American Ricky Bryan.

Bryan, who died of a heart attack at age 47, was a favorite son in his hometown of Coweta, Okla., and a favorite of Switzer.

"Just a great kid – a great old country boy," Switzer said.

Tater Hill. That was the nickname Switzer gave Bryan during the recruiting process because the strapping farm lad (How many people do you know who can hold two square hay bales with one hand?) hailed from the Coweta "suburb" of Tater Hill.

Switzer was wasting his time recruiting Tater Hill. Bryan and his girlfriend, Shelby, were dead-set on going to Oklahoma State. Bryan's life revolved around agriculture. Oklahoma State was originally known as Oklahoma A&M and the "A"

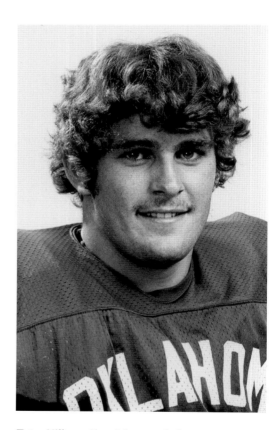

Tater Hill was the nickname Switzer gave Ricky Bryan while recruiting him because Bryan hailed from the Coweta, Okla., "suburb" of the same name. Bryan had been headed to Oklahoma State University before Switzer worked his recruiting magic.

"My profession was all about relationships in the end, anyway. That's really what it was about. It's not about championships and wins and games and all that. ... When you recruit a player, you have got them for life."

— *Barry Switzer*

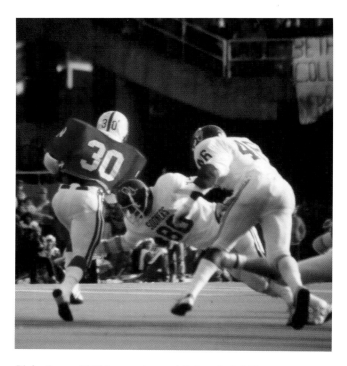

Ricky Bryan (80) lunges toward Nebraska's Mike Rozier (30) during a game on Nov. 26, 1982. Bryan made 365 tackles during his years as a Sooner, 1980-83.

stood for "agricultural."

Said Shelby, who later became Mrs. Tater Hill, "If someone would have told Ricky, 'You are going to be going to OU,' he would have thought that was the biggest joke you ever heard."

What happened?

Shelby said Switzer turned on the good-old-boy charm and worked magic.

"Ricky's dad had a great influence on Ricky and coach Switzer came and he just made himself at home and sat down at their kitchen table and had biscuits and gravy that Ricky's mother prepared," Shelby said. "After he visits, it looks like we are headed to OU."

Switzer has a reputation for sparking two-way loyalty. He was so loyal to others during his coaching career that it sometimes came back to bite him. And he had a gift for inspiring fierce loyalty in his players. After the newlywed situation, how could the Bryans not be loyal to Switzer?

Shelby, protective of Switzer, would not have told this story except the coach told it himself in "Bootlegger's Boy," his 1990 autobiography.

Ricky and Shelby had just gotten married. Two weeks later, they returned to their Norman apartment and were astonished by what they saw, which was a lot of nothing. They had been burglarized.

"It had just been ransacked," she said. "They took everything. Even the phone on the wall was gone. All of our brand new wedding gifts (some not opened) were gone. ... I had purchased cleaning supplies and they even took the cleaning supplies."

The newlyweds were devastated. They were broke college kids. How were they going to survive?

"Ricky was crying," she said. "I was crying. We didn't know what to do."

Their search for a solution led them to Switzer.

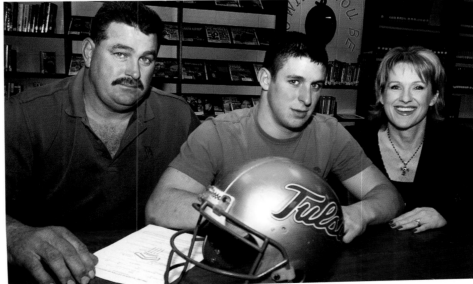

(Top) Ricky Bryan is shown during the Nebraska game in 1982. (Below) Ricky Bryan, former OU and Atlanta Falcons defensive tackle, and his wife, Shelby, are shown with their son, Coweta High School linebacker Mike Bryan (center). Mike Bryan signed a letter of intent to play football for the University of Tulsa in 2006.

In his first year as head coach, Barry Switzer speaks to brothers Lee Roy Selmon (93) and Dewey Selmon (91) during the University of Oklahoma-Miami game on Oct. 6, 1973.

"We go to his office and it was just like talking to your daddy," Shelby said. "He told us, 'It's going to be OK. We're going to get everything replaced.' He had a heart. He had so much empathy for his players."

Shelby said Switzer made a phone call and had the apartment restocked.

"Obviously the NCAA today would shoot you (for doing that)," former OU assistant coach Merv Johnson said. "But that's the way Barry was."

Shelby shouldn't have been surprised. When she arrived in Norman after two years of junior college, Switzer took a personal interest in making sure she got enrolled in classes.

"He had so many irons in the fire and he did so much more than recruiting and

"I guarantee you there's not a soul in Oklahoma who has given as many eulogies as Barry Switzer has. And unfortunately, way too many of them have been former players."

— *Merv Johnson, former assistant coach and later director of football operations and radio color commentator for OU*

coaching," she said. "He cared for his players and their wives and girlfriends."

Said Switzer during a 2007 interview with the Tulsa World: "My profession was all about relationships in the end anyway. That's really what it was about. It's not about championships and wins and games and all that. It's about relationships, certainly the college game is. Those are the guys that you make a difference in their lives and, when you recruit a player, you have got them for life."

Caring is what made Switzer a successful coach, according to Bobby Warmack, who played quarterback at Oklahoma when Switzer was an assistant in the 1960s. College football was, and is, big business. Switzer made it personal.

> "He doesn't just remember me. He knows my number. He can tell you about five or six events in my career that stick out that he has got filed away. He can tell you my parents' names."
>
> — *Former offensive lineman Jon Phillips*

"Barry has got great recall of names and people and players, whether you were a starter or whether you were holding dummies for the scout team," Warmack said. "He knew who you were and where you were from. ... That's just an indication that he really cared about the players and he loved them and that never went away. Years later, when you left the university if you ever needed any help or if you needed anything, Barry was the one that you could call and know that he would be there and be supportive and he would help you and I know that he has done that for many players down through the years."

Those who know Switzer marvel at his ability to recall the names of former players. Want to perfect facial recognition software? Tap into Switzer's brain.

"He doesn't just remember me," former offensive lineman Jon Phillips said. "He knows my number. He can tell you about

Billy Sims Wins Heisman Trophy

By BILL CONNORS
World Sports Editor

Suite 114 at the University of Oklahoma's Bud Wilkinson Complex had its second occupant reach college football's summit Tuesday when halfback Billy Sims won the Heisman Memorial Trophy as the nation's outstanding college player of 1978.

Sims' roommate, offensive guard Greg Roberts, was named winner of the Outland Trophy Saturday, a honor bestowed on the nation's outstanding interior lineman.

It was only the third time in history the award winners were teammates, but the second year in a row

Related news on C-1

Fullback Earl Campbell and tackle Brad Shearer of Texas swept the honors in 1977. Nebraska flanker Johnny Rodgers and guard Rich Glover were the first pair of teammates to be honored, in 1972.

Sims and Roberts are the first roommates to sweep the awards. "I'd like to think something like this probably could only happen at Oklahoma," Coach Barry Switzer said.

Sims and Roberts, who met as Texas schoolboys when they were recruited by OU in 1975, have roomed together for four years. They figure they are indebted to each other.

"If Greg wasn't such a great blocker I wouldn't have gained enough yards to win the Heisman," Sims said, "and he thinks if I hadn't gained so many yards he wouldn't have gotten the recognition to win the Outland."

Sims is from Hooks, Texas; Roberts from Nacogdoches, Texas.

Sims, 205-pound junior who led the nation in rushing and scoring and set a Big Eight Conference record by gaining 1,762 yards, won narrowly over Penn State quarterback Chuck Fusina. Fusina had 163 first place votes to 151 for Sims. But Sims had more second and third place votes thus shading Fusina in points, 827-750.

Michigan quarterback Rick Leach was third with 435 points. Southern California tailback Charles White was fourth with 354 points.

Sims' winning margin was the smallest in 20 years. A ballot recount was ordered before the sponsoring Downtown Athletic Club of New York announced Sims was the winner. The voting is done by sports writers from eight regions, each of which has an equal number of votes.

Sims will receive the bronze trophy at a dinner in New York on Dec. 7.

The day Sims signed a national letter of intent with Oklahoma in 1975, following a fabled high school career, he said his goals were to letter as a freshman, start as a sophomore, make All-America as a junior and win the Heisman as a senior.

His timetable was thrown off schedule by a shoulder injury that forced him to the sidelines in 1976 (A hardship ruling by the Big Eight Conference allowed him an additional year of eligibility). Thus, he wound up winning the Heisman one year ahead of schedule.

Although considered a favorite since setting a national collegiate record by gaining over 200 yards in three straight games at midseason, Sims thought his fumble in the closing minutes of OU's 17-14 loss to Nebraska would keep him from winning the Heisman.

"I thought Leach would win it," Sims said Tuesday. "But I am very happy I was wrong. This is something every football player dreams of."

Sims is the third OU player to win the Heisman, and only the sixth junior since the award was instituted in 1935, as a monument to John W. Heisman. Heisman was an imaginative coach at Georgia Tech, Rice, Auburn, Clemson and other colleges who had a profound influence on the game's development.

Halfback Billy Vessels was OU's first Heisman winner, in 1952. Tailback Steve Owens won in 1969. Vessels and Owens, like 36 of the other Heisman winners, were seniors.

The five juniors who preceded Sims were Doc Blanchard, Army, 1945; Doak Walker, Southern Methodist, 1948; Vic Janowicz, Ohio State, 1950; Roger Staubach, Navy, 1963, and Archie Griffin, Ohio State, 1974. Only Griffin repeated as a senior

Plan to Kill Officials Revealed

Cost of Living Posts Another Sharp Gain

MEMPHIS, Tenn. (AP) — Author-lawyer Mark Lane said Tuesday there is a "master plan" to murder high U.S. government officials, defectors from the Peoples Temple and columnists who have written critically of the sect.

Lane told ABC News that he learned of the plan from a woman identified only as the second in command to sect leader Rev. Jim Jones. Lane said the plan is financed with

From World Wire Reports
WASHINGTON — Sparked by sharp increases in food and housing prices, the cost of living soared 8 percent in October — and has more than doubled in the past 11 years, the Department of Labor reported Tuesday.

"It's God awful," said Alfred E. Kahn, the plain-talking chairman of the White House Council on Wage and Price Stability.

The department's figures showed that consumer prices have doubled since 1967, meaning that the dollar buys only half as much as it did then. A basket of goods that cost $10 in 1967 was priced at $20.07 last month

LAST MONTH'S PRICE SURGE "confirms the fact that we have a very stubborn inflation problem to deal with," White House press secre-

tary Jody Powell said of the report. "It underscores the importance of bringing in a very tight and restrained 1980 budget in January, which the president intends to do."

"It also underscores the necessity of strong support from Congress, from business and from labor" for the Carter administration's voluntary program to fight inflation, Powell said.

Kahn, who is directing the anti-in-

The lead story on the front page of the Tulsa World on Nov. 29, 1978, informed readers that University of Oklahoma running back Billy Sims had won the Heisman Trophy. Sims led the Sooners to an 11-1 record and an Orange Bowl victory over Nebraska. He is OU's all-time career rushing leader with 4,118 yards from 1975-79.

Barry Switzer speaks to his team in the Legends Flag Football Game in April 2009. Former OU players including Brian Bosworth, Tony Casillas and Joe Washington played in the game, which preceded the annual Red/White Scrimmage.

five or six events in my career that stick out that he has got filed away. He can tell you my parents' names."

Warmack recalled an instance at a spring game when someone lost a roster of former players who were going to be introduced over the public address system. Switzer to the rescue. He instantly recognized players and rattled off stories about them.

"He got stumped on one guy that played in the 1950s," Warmack said. "And he only got stumped for a little bit."

Former player Eddie Hinton has a story on the subject of Switzer's recall.

In 2005, Billy Sims sweet-talked Switzer into attending a reunion of former players in Houston. The intent of the reunion was to honor Switzer, who was reluctant to appear. Sims hooked him with these words: "Coach, you still owe me one."

Many "name" players talked about the impact Switzer had on their lives. And then ...

"This guy gets up and nobody knew him," Hinton said. "Warmack and I were sitting together and I said, 'Who's this cat, man?' I haven't ever seen him. Well, he held the (practice) dummies and Barry had kept up with him all through his career and college when he graduated and he went to Texas and became a lawyer. He said, 'I could not believe that every time he came down here, he would always call me.' ... Barry has got this incredible mind that he can tell you what the kid is doing and what he did and where he is today."

Former OU assistant coach Larry Lacewell described Switzer as a walking telephone book.

"He can remember my telephone number back when I was a kid in high school in Fordyce (Ark.)," Lacewell said. "He has al-

"If we would have had cell phones back then, he would have recruited every human being in America. ... "He stopped at every pay phone known to mankind and called recruits."

— Former OU assistant coach Larry Lacewell

ways had that ability. He is a numbers guy, much more so than people would imagine. He has got a Rolodex of people's names, events and whatever in his head."

Think that came in handy during recruiting?

"If we would have had cell phones back then, he would have recruited every human being in America," Lacewell said. "He stopped at every pay phone known to mankind and called recruits."

Tater Hill was a recruit Switzer shouldn't have been able to snare. Years after Bryan's college and NFL career was over, he returned to Norman in the spring for a Red/White Scrimmage and shared stories with Switzer afterward. Shelby eavesdropped and was wowed that Switzer remembered specifics of plays going all the way back to her husband's freshman season.

"They just laughed and talked," she said. "It was awesome. I just sat and listened."

When Bryan lost his life way too soon, Switzer immediately showed up in Coweta with former OU assistants in tow. Bryan had been to Norman a few weeks earlier to tape some interviews and he had autographed an OU helmet which was going to be used for charity purposes. Switzer, broken-hearted, gave the helmet to Ricky's family.

"It was just one of those raw, all-touching moments," Shelby said. "It sent such a message of what they thought of Ricky and just what human people they are."

A memorial service at Coweta High School was scheduled on a Thursday at 10 a.m. Problem: A memorial service for Switzer's first college coach, former OU All-American Jack Mitchell, was scheduled three hours later on the same day at First Freewill Baptist Church in Wellington, Kan.. For all of Switzer's talents, not even he could be in two places at once. But, with the help of police escorts, Switzer zigged to Coweta and zagged to Tulsa, where he hopped on a plane to get to Wellington.

"I guarantee you there's not a soul in Oklahoma who has given as many eulogies as Barry Switzer has," Johnson said. "And, unfortunately, way too many of them have been former players."

Former Sooner Thomas Lott said Switzer doesn't show up at memorial services because he feels obligated to do so.

"In his heart, he is drawn to help the people that have been around him and have done things for him and helped make his success," the Oklahoma quarterback said. "None of us are successful without great people around us. He is no different. He has had great people around him and he honors that."

That Tater Hill nickname Switzer issued to Bryan? It was given to a country boy by a country boy.

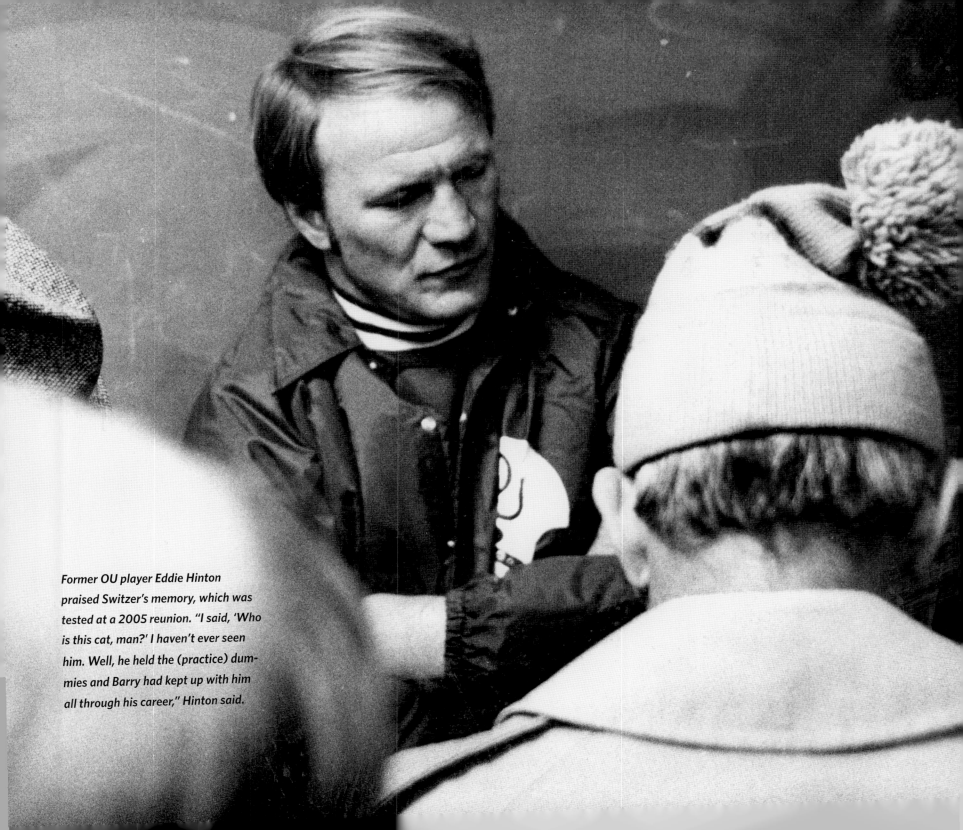

Former OU player Eddie Hinton
praised Switzer's memory, which was
tested at a 2005 reunion. "I said, 'Who
is this cat, man?' I haven't ever seen
him. Well, he held the (practice) dummies and Barry had kept up with him
all through his career," Hinton said.

CHAPTER 2

Crossett

"Barry's daddy couldn't exhibit any wealth. He was hiding his (bootlegging) money in tin cans. And I go to the house and it looked like a haunted house. ... And I said 'Good gosh, this guy is poorer than me.' "

— *Larry Lacewell, former OU assistant coach*

Opposite: Crossett High School football team co-captains Barry Switzer (center) and Jimmy Gadberry model rain jackets donated to their high school football team by W.B. Anderson.

SON OF A BOOTLEGGER

Switzer shows off a fish in 1940.

B arry Switzer was Oklahoma's offensive coordinator in 1971, when the Sooner wishbone gutted defenses for an NCAA-record 5,196 rushing yards.

That's about how many yards Crossett, Ark., is from the northern border of Louisiana.

You won't find a "home of Barry Switzer" sign near any of the roads which trickle into Crossett, where Switzer spent his childhood years. But Billy Joe Holder said there has been talk of naming a street after his longtime friend.

And why not? Only three men on the planet have coached teams to a college football national championship and a Super Bowl title. Switzer, who grew up in a "shotgun" house a few miles southwest of Crossett, is in that exclusive club.

Among signs travelers will see as they enter town: The obligatory population (5,507) sign and another that reads "Welcome to Crossett, the Timber Capital of the South."

It's not false bravado. Crossett was built on wood.

Logging trucks are a common sight in this neck of southern Arkansas. Roads are walled off by pine trees so tall that, as far as strangers know, the next town

"My daddy was good-looking. He got shot by a 28-year-old woman, his girlfriend, when he was 64."

— *Barry Switzer*

"Hunting" with his father, Frank, in 1940.

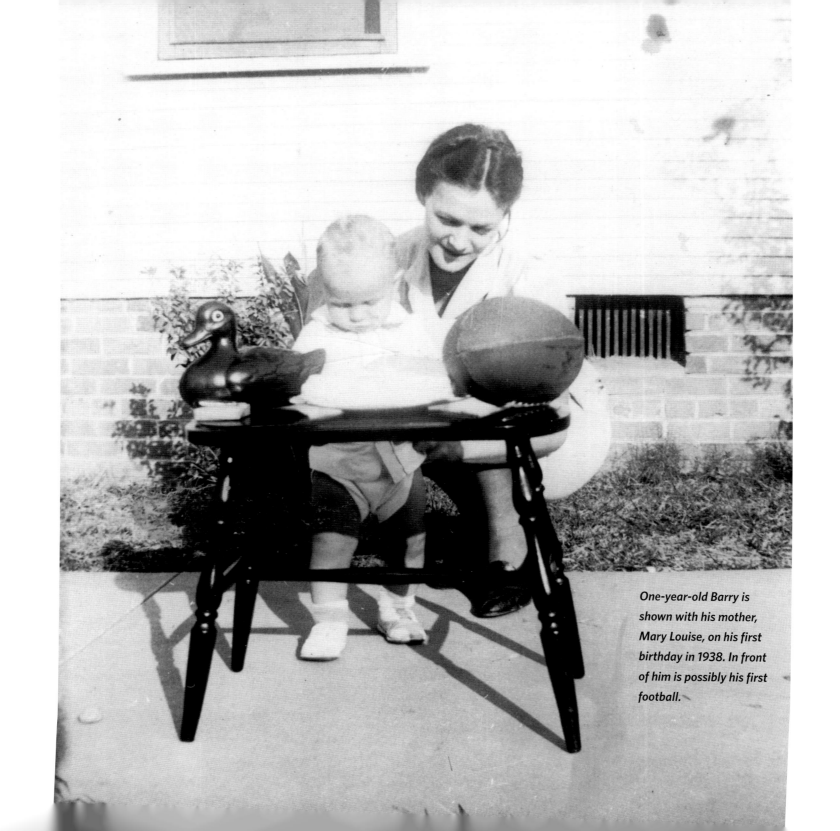

One-year-old Barry is shown with his mother, Mary Louise, on his first birthday in 1938. In front of him is possibly his first football.

could be just around the bend or it could be forests away.

At the end of the 19th century, Crossett Lumber Company saw all that timber and simultaneously saw dollar signs. A town sprang up. Tents for workers were replaced by houses constructed, maintained and owned by the company, according to R.R. Reynolds, who authored "The Crossett Story" for the U.S. Department of Agriculture Forest Service.

Crossett is located in Ashley County which was, and still is, a dry county. If you wanted alcohol, you could visit bootleggers on the outskirts of town. One of them was Frank Switzer, the father of Barry Switzer.

Crossett, Ark., is a town of about 5,500 people and once was known as the "Timber Capital of the South." The building that once housed a pool hall where Switzer and his friends hung out is now the Crossett Service Company, a heating and air conditioning firm.

There's no Barry Switzer sign in Crossett, but don't take that to mean the town isn't proud of the bootlegger's kid.

A big shindig – Barry Switzer Appreciation Day – was held at the Rose Inn in Crossett in 1960, after Switzer had become a hometown hero for the state's beloved Arkansas Razorbacks.

The Rose Inn was a hotel built by the lumber company to house overnight visitors to Crossett and, according to historical accounts, third-floor rooms were reserved for single school teachers. Different times.

The Rose Inn doesn't exist anymore. Centennial Park rests on the site where the hotel once stood. Also gone is a movie theater where Switzer and his boyhood pals watched westerns on Saturdays.

A chunk of Switzer's youth was spent shooting pool and playing moon (a domino game) at the pool hall. That building still stands, but now it houses Crossett Service Company, LLC.

"I have people walk in all the time and say my favorite pool table was right there," said Virginia Turner from her seat just inside the front door.

There are still familiar "things" in Crossett. One of them is Billy Joe Holder, who lives on Cedar Street.

Resting on a shelf in Holder's living room is an autographed OU football. "To Bill Holder. My best friend – love you!! Barry Switzer. 157-29-4." (The numbers? Switzer's record as the Sooners' head coach.)

Holder pulls out his autographed copy of "Bootlegger's Boy." Written on the inside cover: "Billy – Just simply love you – Barry. 157-29-4."

Photographs (many featuring Switzer or former OU players) on Holder's refrigerator become conversation topics when others visit his home.

"My son had an accident," Holder said, after pointing out his son in a photo. "He was paralyzed in a wheelchair and turned over and hit his head on the concrete. His funeral was just a few days after Barry had back surgery. I told Barry not to come. Sure enough, he got on a plane and came to the funeral. That's just how he is."

> "My son had an accident. ... His funeral was just a few days after Barry had back surgery. I told Barry not to come. Sure enough, he got on a plane and came to the funeral. That's just how he is."
>
> — *Billy Joe Holder, longtime Switzer friend*

Does Switzer ever make his way back to Crossett? Holder underwent stomach surgery in 2014 and, after being released from the hospital, got a surprise visit from his buddy.

"I was in here fooling with the computer and I walked in the kitchen and there he stood," Holder said. "He flew down to check on me. He told my wife he was coming and told her not to tell me."

Holder said he and Switzer have been running around together ever since they "hit it off" in the eighth grade. In subsequent years, Switzer may have spent more time (and eaten more meals) at Holder's house than his own house.

"We were always together, kind of

Billy Joe Holder displays books autographed by Switzer at Holder's home in Crossett, Ark. The book inscriptions read, "Billy – My best friend from a lucky S.O.B . – Barry Switzer" and "Billy – Just simply love you – Barry 157-29-4."

Barry, age 2, during a family visit in El Dorado, Ark.

A portrait of Barry Switzer at age 3 in 1940.

Switzer wears a cowboy outfit on his fourth birthday in 1941.

Barry at age 12 in a school photo.

like truck and trailer," Holder said.

Boys will be boys? They weren't opposed to eating a stolen watermelon or trekking to Bastrop, La., to drink beer.

"There wasn't a lot to do here," Holder said. "Whatever we did, we made it fun."

Holder smiles when he talks about how they were crazy enough to wade chest-deep into Crossett's Mud Lake to go fishing, never mind snapping turtles, snakes or whatever else might be lurking about.

"We wouldn't do that now for nothing," he said.

Snakes were apparently a hazard at other spots around Crossett.

Switzer said in a 1976 Sports Illustrated article and repeated in his book that he used to carry a pistol in case he needed to shoot copperheads while escorting his mother to a three-hole "privy" behind his childhood home.

Switzer told SI his grandfather planted tomatoes behind the outhouse and they were the "best darned tomatoes in the county." Switzer's home was far from the best in the county.

"Hey, I thought I was poor 'til I visited Barry," Fordyce, Ark., native and long-time friend Larry Lacewell told SI in 1976.

Asked for details in 2014, Lacewell said, "Barry was a bootlegger's boy and he lived out in an area that we called Blacktown. I went to spend the night. Barry's daddy couldn't exhibit any wealth. He was hiding his (bootlegging) money in tin cans. And I go to the house and it looked like a haunted house. It had netting. You would put your wallpaper up that sticks to it and it's not even wallpaper. It looks like mosquito netting. And I said, 'Good gosh, this guy is poorer than me' – which was probably wrong really because he had a lot of tin cans out there and there weren't any tin cans at my house."

Barry (63) as a sophomore on his high school football team in 1953.

Detailing his background for the Oklahoma oral history website *voicesofoklahoma.com*, Switzer told interviewer John Erling his childhood home was built at least three feet off the ground.

"I always thought shotgun houses were built so the dogs, cats, hogs and chickens had to have a place to live," Switzer said. "But it was called a shotgun house because you could shoot a shotgun through the front door out the back door and you wouldn't hit anyone unless someone happened to be walking across the house from one room to another room."

Longtime friend Jim Mooty of El Dorado, Ark., said you could almost see through Switzer's house.

A school portrait of Barry as a high school junior in 1954.

"This being the Bible Belt, the Baptists more or less didn't want their daughters dating Barry because his dad was a bootlegger."

— *Billy Joe Holder, longtime Switzer friend*

"But you know what?" Mooty said. "A lot of people were like that during those days. It wasn't any fault of Barry's. But he grew up the hard way."

Lacewell suggested Switzer was more socially poor than financially poor.

"What I mean by that is, in small towns, if you were the bootlegger's son, you weren't exactly on everybody's dance card," Lacewell said. "So I think he suffered from that and wanting to prove people wrong."

"This being the Bible Belt, the Baptists more or less didn't want their daughters dating Barry because his dad was a bootlegger," Holder said. "But we got around that. We had somebody pick a girl up and take her on out."

Switzer gained popularity despite social stigma. The school yearbook in the lumber company town was called "The Termite." Check out the 1955 Termite and you'll see a page dedicated to senior football stars, with a photo of "Captain Barry Switzer" anchoring the center of the page. You'll also find a photo of Switzer crowning homecoming queen Deanna Atkins and another photo of him beaming while modeling (with football co-captain Jimmy Gadberry) donated football rain jackets.

Switzer was the state's high school lineman of the year as a senior. He wrote in his book that his father did not get to see him play a game that season. Bootlegging had caught up with Frank Switzer, who was serving prison time.

Frank died on Nov. 16, 1972, only a few months before Barry was chosen to suc-

Barry (63) and Jimmy Gadberry escort homecoming queen Deanna Atkins in 1954.

ceed Chuck Fairbanks. Barry told reporters he wished his daddy had lived long enough to see him become the head coach at Oklahoma.

In 1972, Frank's death played out in the news as an accident. A United Press International report said Lulu Dawkins (called Lula Mae Dawkins in "Bootlegger's Boy") accidentally shot Frank as she attempted to remove a gun from her car at his home. She was driving him to Crossett for medical treatment when her car hit a power pole and burst into flames.

Only the last part is true. The shooting was no accident and the shooter was a jealous lover.

"My daddy was good-looking," Barry said during a 2012 interview with the Tulsa World's Bill Haisten, comparing Frank to Rhett Butler in "Gone With The Wind."

"He got shot by a 28-year-old woman, his girlfriend, when he was 64. If he hadn't gotten shot, he'd be alive today. He was jogging during the '50s before anyone else was doing it. He had an old pair of black Converse high-tops and he jogged down the

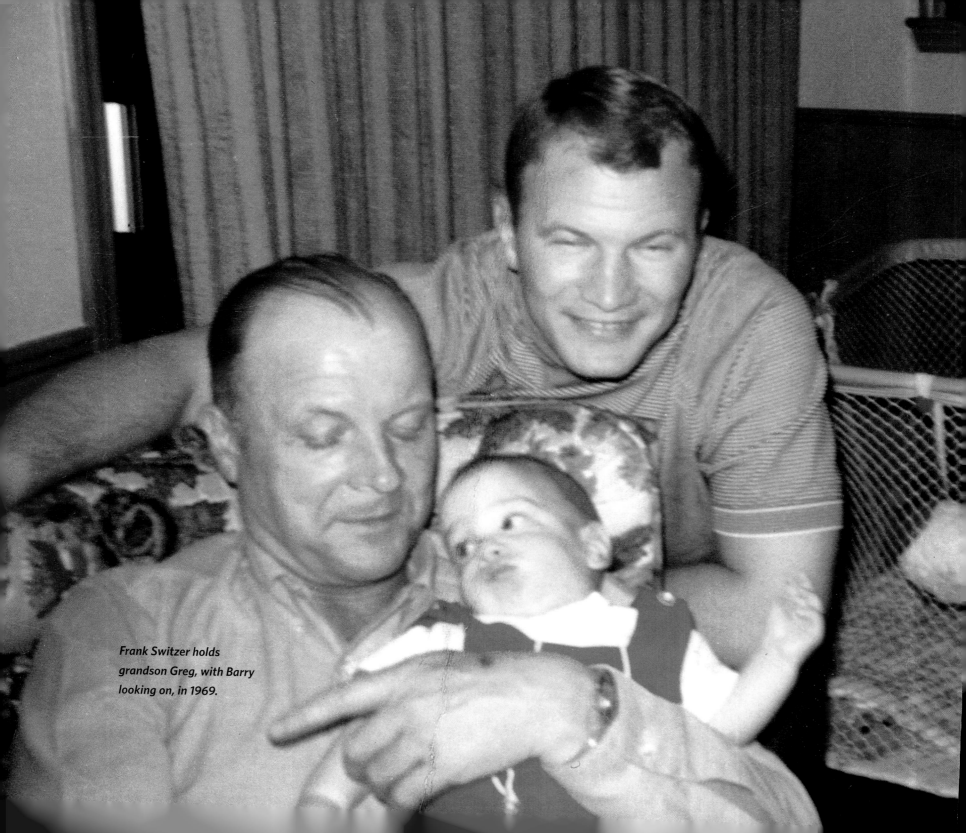

Frank Switzer holds grandson Greg, with Barry looking on, in 1969.

gravel roads."

Frank used to climb a rope which dangled from a big tree in the yard. The tree is gone. So is his last house, lost to a fire a few years ago, according to Ovid Switzer, a cousin who said he has lived on the family property for close to 40 years.

A wild turkey strolled through the yard as Ovid was talking. He grabbed the turkey, cradled it and continued talking.

"These roosters get to fighting out here and the turkey will break them up," Ovid said. "He's my official."

A gravel road once ran in front of the old Switzer place. The road is paved now and it passes near where Frank is buried. A dirt road through the woods provides the only automobile access to Macedonia Cemetery. It's a small cemetery with only a few headstones, many marking the graves of Switzers.

In April, Frank's grave had been decorated with an Easter-themed arrangement. Standing graveside, Holder said, "Barry certainly thought a lot of his daddy."

Holder said Barry resembles his father, even in body structure. Both can be hard to categorize. Holder said Frank was tough and gentle at the same time.

"People didn't know about it, but Frank sent a lot of black kids to college," Holder said, adding that Frank purchased groceries and other items for needy people. Store owners were instructed to let them have what they wanted with an agreement

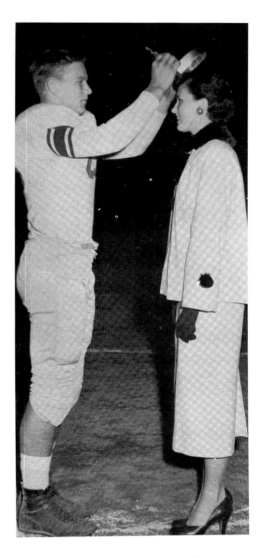

Barry crowns homecoming queen Deanna Atkins in Crossett, Ark., in 1954.

that Frank would come by to settle the bill later.

"One time Barry came down and he had done won a couple of national championships," Holder said. "We went to a boot-legger's to get a beer. We went out to this section of town, a black section. Barry asked him, 'Do you know who I am?' He said, 'Yeah, you are Mr. Frank's boy.' He knew he was coaching the Oklahoma Sooners, but he knew him as Mr. Frank's boy. And he wouldn't let him pay for the beer because he was Mr. Frank's boy."

A padlocked gate guards the road to the cemetery. Frank's resting place is protected by natural guardians. Barry once visited the cemetery while in town for a class reunion and got "eaten up" by red bugs. For relief, he took a bath in chigger-killing chemicals.

Holder (wearing a 1984 Big Eight championship ring) said Barry does not forget old buddies. They've gone to Las Vegas together and have taken fishing rods all over the globe. Once, while fishing with celebrity outdoorsman Jimmy Houston, one of the "amateurs" got a strike, but the hook came back empty. When Houston cast his line in the same spot, Switzer said this to Holder: "He ain't no different than us."

Holder initially turned down an invitation to accompany Switzer to New York City when the coach made it into the College Football Hall of Fame. But Holder got sweet-talked into going and the good old boys from Crossett, separated in age by only six days, had a great time in the nation's biggest city.

Asked if Switzer always succeeds at persuasion, Holder said, "He don't miss much. He is in the high 90 percent."

Opposite: The headstone of Barry Switzer's father, Frank, stands in the secluded Switzer family burial grounds near Crossett, Ark. Frank Switzer, a boot-legger, died only a few months before Barry was chosen to succeed Chuck Fairbanks as head coach at Oklahoma.

CHAPTER 3

Fayetteville

" ... and I had told her that I would rather know that I would never see her again the rest of my life and know that she was safe and taken care of (than see her) in the condition that she was in. And my mother walked outside and took a gun and shot and killed herself."

— *Barry Switzer*

Switzer was extremely shy as a freshman at the University of Arkansas, friends said. After about a year and a half, the real Barry — the one with charisma — started to come out. "He was just a tremendous leader," said teammate Jim Mooty. "Everybody respected and liked Barry."

FINDING HIS VOICE

Switzer is shown with a member of Arkansas' coaching staff in 1958. His friend and teammate Jim Mooty said of Switzer: "He could tell you things about the team we were fixing to play ... He would have already figured those dudes out. He was just very knowledgeable about the game, even at a young age."

B elieve it or not, Barry Switzer was an introvert when he showed up to play football for the University of Arkansas.

"You wouldn't know it today," former teammate Bill Michael said. "But ... he was one of the most humble guys and most shy guys I believe I have ever known."

Michael first encountered another shy kid from Crossett.

Freddy Gill, from the same hometown as Switzer, shared a dorm with Michael when Switzer was a Razorback rookie. Gill was so quiet that Michael kidded him that they probably should talk to each other once in a while since, you know, they were roommates.

"And Switzer was worse than he was," Michael said. "I don't think Switzer said 'Hi' more than twice for about two or three weeks."

Longtime Switzer pal Larry Lacewell, who played at Arkansas A&M, backs up Michael's claim that Switzer was extremely shy. Lacewell said Switzer displayed skills in college, but talking was not one of them.

"That was my skill," Lacewell said. "He loved to listen to me, even back when we were kids. I would tell stories to him back then about how great I

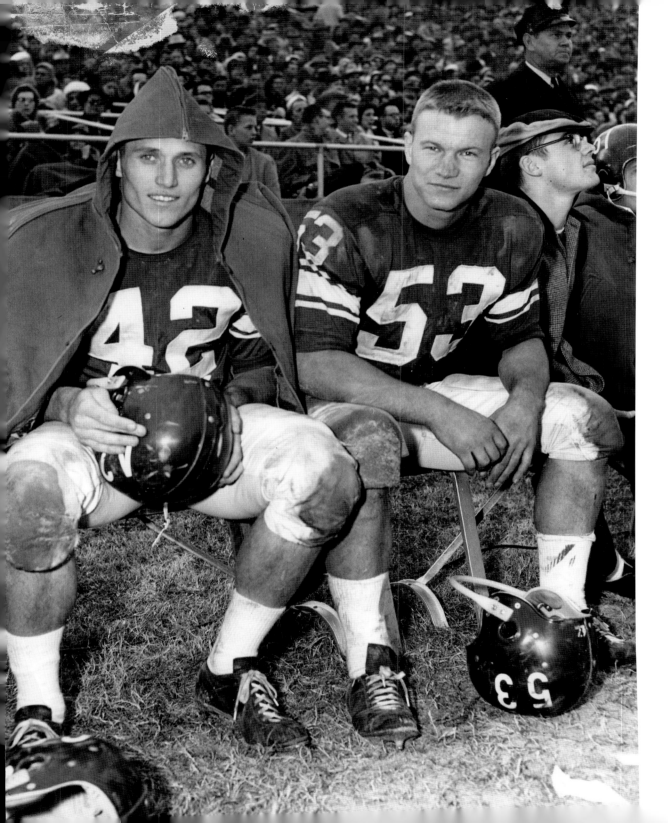

Switzer (53), with Arkansas halfback Donnie Stone during their Oct. 26, 1957, game against Ole Miss. "No one really knew that my daddy was a bootlegger and he was in prison in the Arkansas State Penitentiary. ... No one held me accountable for all that. But it drove me. I wanted to bust my butt. I didn't want to be a failure," Switzer said in a 2007 interview.

Switzer (left), future University of Texas head coach Fred Akers and Jim Hollander clown around in the locker room at the University of Arkansas in 1959.

was. He got a kick out of listening to me."

Lacewell wondered if Switzer would last in Fayetteville. Switzer often hitchhiked to Arkansas A&M to spend time with hometown buddies such as Billy Joe Holder, who was Lacewell's college suitemate. Switzer wasn't getting to play for the Razorbacks. But his friends were immediately playing for the Boll Weevils. Would he join them in Monticello?

Maybe it was a good sign when Switzer (who headed to college with only a few possessions) felt comfortable enough in Fayetteville to borrow blue jeans and white T-shirts from teammates.

"That's what we all wore to class every day," Michael said. "But his didn't fit him near as well as ours fit us. They were so dang tight on him he looked like he was going to pop out of them. After he got to know us a little better, he would take our clothes and wear them if his happened to be dirty."

Switzer was an alpha male under Friday night lights in Crossett. He was just another male when he showed up in Fayetteville.

"I was an average player," he said in a 2007 interview with the Tulsa World. "Everybody else was just as good as I was. But the only way I could separate myself from the rest of them was I was smart, I didn't make mistakes and I knew what to do and I busted my rear end and hustled. The only reason I got to play is they knew I would give effort. Coaches recognize effort. That maybe separated me from a bunch of guys who were as good or better than I was."

Merv Johnson was hired as a graduate assistant at Arkansas in 1958, when Switzer was a junior. Johnson described Switzer as a warrior.

"He was one of those country tough guys," Johnson said. "He could take a pounding and he could dish it out. He loved to play."

Johnson said other players recognized Switzer's qualities and decided he is someone you want in your foxhole.

"He was just a tremendous leader," former teammate Jim Mooty said. "Everybody respected and liked Barry."

Switzer was chosen a tri-captain as a senior in 1959, helping the Hogs go 9-2 and share a Southwest Conference championship. Football players weren't huge in that era, but he played center at 190 pounds and had something to prove.

"No one really knew that my daddy was a bootlegger and he was in prison in the Arkansas State Penitentiary," Switzer said in 2007. "I look back on it now and I think about it and it's ridiculous anyway. No one would have given a damn anyway or cared. No one held me accountable for all that. But it drove me. I wanted to bust my butt. I didn't want to be a failure. It kept me from being a failure. It was a driving force that I wanted to prove I could be successful because I knew some people would say, 'Well, he'll

> "He was one of those country tough guys. He could take a pounding and he could dish it out. He loved to play."
>
> — *Merv Johnson, graduate assistant at Arkansas when Switzer was a player*

wind up in prison too.' "

College football was in the midst of a one-platoon era during Switzer's college career, in which players played both offense and defense and a second unit was deployed to combat fatigue, but a "wild card" rule allowed for one substitution per down. Frank Broyles, Arkansas' coach during Switzer's final two seasons, used the wild card to play Wayne Harris at linebacker on "Big Red" and "Wild Hog" units (the first and second teams). He chose Switzer to man the center position for both.

Barry Switzer attended the University of Arkansas from 1956-60 on an athletic scholarship. He played center and linebacker for the Razorbacks. Switzer (53) is shown in 1959 during his senior year, when he was one of the team's three captains.

Harris became an All-American in 1960 and played well enough in Canada to gain a spot in the Canadian Football League Hall of Fame. Small world? Harris played high school ball in El Dorado, Ark., about 40 miles west of Crossett. Mooty, an All-America halfback in 1959, was from El Dorado, where Switzer attended school for two years while his parents were separated.

Opposite: Jim Mooty (24), scoots 20 yards for the game-winning touchdown in the Gator Bowl game at Jacksonville, Fla., on Jan. 2, 1960. Mooty rushed 18 times for 99 yards as Arkansas defeated Georgia Tech, 14-7.

Jim Mooty, an all-American halfback from El Dorado, Ark., and Switzer knew each other as teenagers. Mooty once warned Switzer to stay away from the girls in El Dorado. They became friends in college and Switzer led an effort to reinstate Mooty after he had temporarily left the team.

Mooty recalled that Switzer was living in Crossett when they had an encounter at a teen hangout in El Dorado. Mooty issued this warning: "I told him, 'You need to stay in Crossett. You need to leave our girls alone up in El Dorado.' "

Mooty says he was just teasing Switzer. They weren't close friends yet, but they became pals in college. There's a funny tale about them in "The Razorbacks," a 1973 book about Arkansas football. Mooty left the team and Broyles let the squad vote on the terms of Mooty's reinstatement. According to the book, Switzer told his teammates this: "Shoot, Mooty doesn't need any spring practice. Let's just bring him back next fall."

To Broyles' astonishment, players voted to approve Switzer's suggestion. But things got hashed out and, after the final game of Switzer's career, reporters heard him shout, "Is that Mooty an All-America?" in the locker room. Mooty rushed 18 times for 99 yards and a winning score in a 14-7 Gator Bowl victory over Georgia Tech.

Meanwhile, Michael watched the once-shy Switzer do a "flip-flop." Michael said football turned Switzer around and Switzer gained a reputation as a ladies' man. He courted a Razorback baton twirler who could blow a duck call so well

Opposite: Switzer (center) and teammates are shown in Fayetteville, Ark., in 1959. "I was an average player," Switzer said in 2007. "... The only reason I got to play is they knew I would give effort. Coaches recognize effort."

that Switzer once had her blow one for a Sports Illustrated reporter who visited his home. "Sure sounds like an oversexed duck to me," Switzer told SI.

Kay McCollum became Mrs. Barry Switzer in 1963, after he became a coach.

Switzer got his first taste of coaching as an Arkansas graduate assistant in 1960. Or was he a "coach" even when he was playing?

"He could tell you things about the team we were fixing to play, like Texas A&M or whoever it was," Mooty said. "He would have already figured those dudes out. He was just very knowledgeable about the game, even at a young age. The rest of us, at our age, we didn't care. We were there to perform."

Tulsa World columnist Bill Connors wrote that Switzer's work as a graduate assistant caught Broyles' eye. Switzer was obligated for military duty after serving as a GA, but Broyles sent word that he wanted Switzer to return to Fayetteville and go to work as an assistant coach. The right strings got pulled and Switzer was granted an early release so he could join the Razorbacks in time to prepare for the 1961 season.

As a graduate assistant, Switzer caught the eye of Arkansas head coach Frank Broyles. Switzer was obligated for military duty, but was granted an early release so he could join the Razorbacks as an assistant coach before the 1961 season.

"After that his career took off," Connors wrote, adding that some in Fayetteville came to view Switzer as a "glib, excitable, fertile-minded carbon copy of Broyles. His enthusiasm and passion for statistics stamped him as unusual."

Connors wrote that Switzer's coaching philosophy was shaped during a 22-game winning streak. Arkansas won 22 in a row from the final game of the 1963 season through the regular season finale in 1965, with a national championship season in between.

The University of Arkansas coaching staff is pictured in 1965, when the team went 10-0 and won the Southwest Conference championship. Pictured are: (front, from left) Johnny Majors, Jim Mackenzie, head coach Frank Broyles, Wilson Matthews and Bill Pace; (back, from left) Steed White, Jack Davis, Barry Switzer, Merv Johnson and Lou Ferrel. The Razorbacks had a 22-game winning streak from the last game of the 1963 season through the regular season finale in 1965, with a national championship in between.

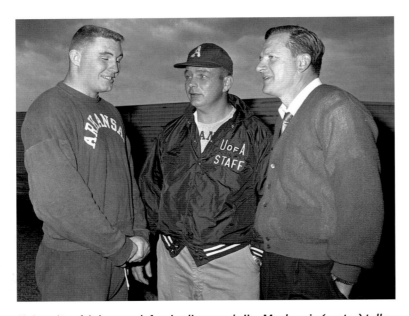

University of Arkansas defensive line coach Jim Mackenzie (center) talks over defensive plays with head coach Frank Broyles (right) and an unidentified player on Dec. 31, 1965, as they wind up practice for their game against Louisiana State University in the Cotton Bowl in Dallas. The photo was taken just after Mackenzie was named as the new head coach for the University of Oklahoma.

During the streak, Switzer was giddy enough to do calendar math and he informed Broyles the Razorbacks were on pace to break Oklahoma's 47-game winning streak in 1968. Broyles chided the young coach for looking so far ahead, but smiled when telling that story to Connors.

During Switzer's years with the Razorbacks, he met the man he would come to call his mentor. That's Jim Mackenzie, who left the Arkansas staff to become Oklahoma's head coach in 1966. Tragedy for Mackenzie was on the horizon and Switzer was not far removed from a horrific tragedy of his own.

Switzer returned to Crossett and visited family members before his senior season in 1959. His mother, Mary Louise Switzer, was a sweet lady who read books all the time, according to Holder.

"One of the last times I saw her, she gave me a book and told me to read it," Holder said.

The book was "Ten North Frederick" by John O'Hara. Holder read it. He said it was a great book. It became the source material for a Gary Cooper movie in 1958.

Switzer wrote in "Bootlegger's Boy" that his mother read books as an escape from a harsh reality. Depressed, she resorted to alcohol.

This is an excerpt of a transcript from a *voicesofoklahoma.com* interview with John Erling:

Said Switzer, "A lot of times I didn't come home at all. I'd go other places because I knew what was at home. But on one occasion, I was at home in the summer while I was in college. I told my mother, she came in one night and I saw the condition that she was in, and I had told her that I would rather know that I would never see her again the rest of my life and know that she was safe and taken care of (than see her) in the condition that she was in."

The transcript reflects that Switzer paused before continuing.

"And my mother walked outside and took a gun and shot and killed herself."

Switzer said in the *voicesofoklahoma.com* interview that he was the last person to talk to his mother and he was the person who picked up his mother and carried her inside the house. He said he stood outside and waited for what seemed like hours for his father, absent during the shooting, to come home.

"And he met me and of course he knew something tragic had happened because he saw the condition that I was in."

Switzer said he bore tremendous guilt for what transpired that night.

"But I've lived my life and I understand that my mother intended to do this," he told Erling. "I hated to see her in the condition that she was in. (My brother) Donnie lived in (that environment) every day and had to live in it longer because he was younger. I was able to escape it and get out of it. I escaped it in high school because … I stayed in town with my friends."

Switzer could have become bitter after Aug. 26, 1959.

"But he didn't," Mooty said, suggesting that his friend was surrounded by many good people through athletics. "He's a very strong individual."

CHAPTER 4

Goathead stickers and a bone

"Jim's death was a low point for me. I never thought it had been a mistake to come to Oklahoma. But for a few days I thought my timing might have been bad. We didn't know who would be the new coach, or if any of us had jobs."

— Barry Switzer

Jim Mackenzie will be remembered for bringing two things to Oklahoma: toughness and Barry Switzer. The OU coaching staff in 1966: (front, from left) Chuck Fairbanks, Pat James, head coach Jim Mackenzie, Homer Rice and Barry Switzer; (back, from left) Ken Rawlinson, Galen Hall, Bill Gray, Swede Lee, Larry Lacewell and Port Robertson.

OUTWORKING AND INNOVATING

"They would take you outside where they didn't know there was a goathead (thorn) patch ... you would have black speckles of broken goatheads in your hands and stuck in your back. At the end of the practice, our tongues were so thick that we couldn't even talk because we had been worked out so hard," said Bobby Warmack, OU quarterback from 1966-68.

I t's 1966. Quarterback Bobby Warmack is among the University of Oklahoma football players at South Base, a Naval training center, to participate in new head coach Jim Mackenzie's offseason conditioning program.

Warmack surveyed the scene at his first fourth quarter class (the nickname for the conditioning program) and noticed trash cans with black plastic liners had been placed around the perimeter of the workout area.

"We were thinking, 'What's this for? Are they going to serve cookies and whatnot after practice and we were going to throw the paper and cups in the trash cans?' " Warmack recalled.

"Well, after 15 or 20 minutes of that fourth quarter class, we found out pretty quick what those trash cans were for. People were upchucking their lunch. ... It wasn't uncommon for everybody to do that. Only the skinny ones like me, who didn't have anything to throw up, wouldn't throw up anything."

Mackenzie will be remembered for bringing two things to OU: toughness and Barry Switzer.

Former player Jim Riley said the Sooners (3-7 the previous season) had gotten soft under the previous regime and needed what Mackenzie brought to the table.

Jim Mackenzie coached only one season at Oklahoma. He died at age 37 of a massive heart attack. His 1966 team finished 6-4 and he was named the Big Eight Coach of the Year by both AP and UPI.

> "The biggest deal was to see how many players could lose weight and we gutted them. It was horrible. Players went through torture. I really mean that."
>
> *— Larry Lacewell,*
> *who joined the OU coaching staff*
> *when Jim Mackenzie was hired*

Larry Lacewell, who joined the OU coaching staff when Mackenzie was hired, said the fourth quarter class was the closest thing to a concentration camp you could imagine.

"The biggest deal was to see how many players could lose weight and we gutted them," Lacewell said. "It was horrible. Players went through torture. I really mean that."

Switzer called it "Stalag 13" and later apologized for what players endured. The Sooners went station to station for an assortment of drills, hustling from one place to the next at every whistle.

"It was about 35 minutes of that, and then we went through 20 or 25 minutes of agility drills," Warmack said. "And they would take you outside where they didn't know there was a goathead (thorn) patch, a sticker patch, and we would do shoulder rolls and (other drills) and you would have black speckles of broken goatheads in your hands and stuck in your back. At the end of the practice, our tongues were so thick that we couldn't even talk because we had been worked out so hard."

Former player Mike Harper said Mackenzie delivered this message before the first fourth quarter class: "Guys, there are about 144 of you here. There are going to be about 45 or so of you left by the time we are through and I don't really care which ones they are."

Some really good players left, according to Harper.

"But they just didn't have, I guess, the heart that Mackenzie wanted them to have," he said. "He didn't want anybody quitting on him and he said if you can get through this, you are not going to quit. We might get beat pretty bad, but you are going to be out there trying."

Mackenzie had played for Paul "Bear" Bryant at Kentucky. Bryant later coached at Texas A&M, and his grueling "Junction Boys" camp of 1954 is part of college football lore.

Pat James, Mackenzie's defensive coordinator at OU, had been at Texas A&M during the Junction Boys experience.

Merv Johnson met Mackenzie at a different school. Said Johnson, "He was my line coach my senior year at Missouri and I hated him. He was the toughest, meanest coach and it was definitely new to us. He was not long out of college and I think he tried to maybe coach like he thought Bear Bryant coached."

Johnson and Mackenzie became staffmates when they served under Frank Broyles at Arkansas. Johnson said Mackenzie "totally changed" in Fayetteville.

"He was smart enough to realize you don't try to copy somebody else," Johnson said. "You take what you learned from other coaches and add it to your personality. Jim was a great guy."

Merv Johnson, whom Mackenzie coached as an assistant at Missouri, said Mackenzie changed his approach at Arkansas. "He was smart enough to realize you don't try to copy somebody else. You take what you learned from other coaches and add it to your personality."

Tulsa World columnist Bill Connors wrote that Mackenzie became an older-brother-type hero to Switzer during their years together at Arkansas. Switzer was ready to tag along if Mackenzie ever got a head coaching job.

"I could sit in a room with 11 other coaches and Jim Mackenzie would say something and it would be the same thing which

"I could sit in a room with 11 other coaches and Jim Mackenzie would say something and it would be the same thing which was going through my mind. I really believed in him and his convictions."

— *Barry Switzer*

was going through my mind," Switzer once told the Tulsa World. "I really believed in him and his convictions."

Mackenzie, of course, got the OU job and hired Switzer. In their first season in Norman, the Sooners went 6-4, beat Texas for the first time in 10 years and handed Nebraska its only regular season defeat. Mackenzie was named the Big Eight's coach of the year. That was also their only season together in Norman.

In April 1967, Mackenzie flew to visit quarterback recruit Monty Johnson in Amarillo, Texas.

Mackenzie experienced chest discomfort during the flight home but seemed fine. Mackenzie and OU assistant Galen Hall lived across the street from each other. A little after midnight, Mackenzie's 12-year-old daughter awakened Hall with the news that something was wrong with her father. Mackenzie had suffered a fatal heart attack. He was 37.

Mackenzie had weight issues. He would go on a crash diet and crash the other way after the diet ran its course. To go from one extreme to another wasn't healthy. And Mackenzie was a heavy smoker, as were many people in that era. But his death at such a young age was a horrible shock.

Connors wrote that Mackenzie's death "almost crushed" Switzer.

"Barry thought that Jim hung the moon," Warmack said. "He was just simply devas-

Sooner offensive coordinator Barry Switzer talks to his players before their Oct. 16, 1971, game against the University of Colorado. Players include Greg Pruitt (30), Tim Welch (45), Grant Burget (25) and Jack Mildren (11).

Chuck Fairbanks was named OU head coach in 1967 following the death of Jim Mackenzie. Fairbanks won three Big Eight Conference titles (1967, 1972 and a shared title in 1968) and was the first OU coach to use the wishbone formation. He left OU to coach in the NFL for the New England Patriots.

tated, as everyone was, but in particular Barry was because of his background with Mackenzie."

Years later, Switzer told the Tulsa World this: "Jim's death was a low point for me. I never thought it had been a mistake to come to Oklahoma. But for a few days I thought my timing might have been bad. We didn't know who would be the new coach, or if any of us had jobs."

OU assistant coaches served as pallbearers at a memorial service in Gary, Ind., where Mackenzie was born. The assistants were at a Holiday Inn in Gary when Chuck Fairbanks was informed by telephone that OU was promoting him to head coach. Though still grieving, the staff could at least breathe a sigh of relief.

"They only gave Chuck an eight-month contract," Switzer told the Tulsa World years later. "But, to us, that was better than nothing."

Harper said Mackenzie could have been at OU "as long as he wanted to be there" if he had lived longer. In Mackenzie's brief stay, he laid a foundation for success, according to Warmack.

One reason Switzer followed Mackenzie to Norman is because Switzer preferred to coach defense. Mackenzie was going to give him that opportunity.

The 1967 Sooner team, with Chuck Fairbanks as head coach and Barry Switzer as offensive coordinator, finished with a 10-1 overall record and went 7-0 in the Big Eight.

Switzer had wanted to coach defense, but things changed after Mackenzie's death. In his third season as offensive coordinator, Switzer called plays for Heisman Trophy winner Steve Owens, shown on Nov. 18, 1969, before the Colorado game.

Switzer coached the offensive line in Mackenzie's lone season and was transitioning to linebackers coach. Fairbanks promoted Switzer to offensive coordinator. Connors wrote that it wasn't what Switzer wanted or what Broyles or Mackenzie had ever envisioned for Switzer.

In his third season as offensive coordinator, Switzer called plays for a Heisman Trophy winner, running back Steve Owens. In Switzer's fourth season as an offensive coordinator, he gambled his future on a wishbone.

OU lost four games in each of the 1968 and 1969 seasons. Three of the losses in '69 were by 30 or more points. Coaches worried they might soon be looking for jobs – and they wouldn't have Owens to saddle and ride in 1970.

Minus Owens, OU switched to a veer offense. In the third game of the 1970 season, the Sooners laid an egg in a 23-14 loss to Oregon State.

"As inexperienced as we were, I knew we had better athletes than Oregon State and should beat them," Switzer said. "Yet, they made us look awful. I was sick."

Two days later – Sept. 26, 1970 – desperation kicked in and a decision was made to junk the veer. A bye week would be used to hastily install the wishbone. The new offense would be unveiled in a fight-fire-with-fire game against top-ranked Texas, which had ridden the wishbone to a national championship the previous season.

Crazy?

"I kind of thought that myself," former offensive line coach Bill Michael said.

Bold?

"I never worried about it being a gamble," Switzer once said. "I just figured I would be on my knees (unemployed) if we didn't do it."

James and Lacewell had been chirping about how hard the wishbone was to defend and, on multiple occasions, they suggested to offensive coaches that they were goofy for not running the 'bone.

Switzer (left) is shown with Steve Owens (center) and OU fullback Mike Harper in September 1969. OU lost four games in each of the 1968 and 1969 seasons, and coaches worried they might soon be looking for jobs.

Said Lacewell: "Well, sure enough, they walk in the room one day on an open date and said, 'We're doing it.' We thought, 'Oh my God. Don't do that. You're crazy.' Anyway we went to it and it became history."

Security was tight at practices and players were told to say nothing about the surprise which awaited Texas.

Greg Pruitt was moved from receiver to halfback (where he became an All-American) when OU changed offenses. The switch initially disappointed him.

Greg Pruitt (left) and Jack Mildren watch from the sidelines during OU's Nov. 13, 1971, game with Kansas.

"I had worked hard to be a starter," he said. "I started as a receiver and then when they switched me to a running back, I went to backup running back to Everett Marshall and they said the reason was they were trying to get me the ball more. I was trying to figure out, 'How do they get me the ball more when I'm standing on the sideline?' "

Jack Mildren also was reluctant to embrace the change in offenses, but his running ability made him an ideal wishbone quarterback.

"Jack was the best," Pruitt said. "At the point of attack he would turn and challenge the defense. Now, when you flip the ball, the defense has got to hesitate and start again. For us, we were fast enough that the split second they hesitate was enough to turn the corner."

If this was a Hollywood tale, Pruitt and Mildren would have sparked an ambush of Texas in the wishbone's maiden voyage. That didn't happen.

"We took the ball and went about 80 yards early in the game and proceeded to get beat bad," Lacewell said, referring to a 41-9 loss in which OU suffered five turnovers. "But you could see what was there. There was a guy that was a federal judge named Frank Seay from Seminole and he called me after the Texas game and said, 'Are you all crazy?' I said, 'Frank, we are on

Sports Section TULSA SUNDAY WORLD Sports Section

TULSA, OKLAHOMA, SUNDAY, OCTOBER 11, 1970

Ump's Call Helps Birds Past Cincy

CINCINNATI (AP)—Veteran third baseman Brooks Robinson gave the Baltimore Orioles the run they needed with a homer and veteran umpire Ken Burkhart made a home-plate call they needed as the Orioles edged Cincinnati, 4-3, Saturday in the opening game of the World Series.

Robinson went only 1-for-19 as the Orioles were upended by the New York Mets in the World Series last year. But he snapped a 3-3 tie in the seventh inning Saturday with a home run that put the finishing flourish on a three-homer Baltimore barrage.

Robinson's homer came only a half inning after the Orioles had gotten the call they needed from Burkhart. That came after Bernie Carbo walked with one out and Tommy Helms followed with a single.

Carbo raced around to third on the play and streaked home when pinch hitter Ty Cline tapped in front of the plate. As Carbo neared the plate, he upended Burkhart while Hendricks lunged for the tag. Burkhart, prone, signaled for the out.

Carbo argued. Cincinnati's Manager Sparky Anderson argued. The crowd of 51,531 howled in derision. Four towels were sailed out of the Reds' dugout.

But the decision stood. And Anderson refused to complain after the game, explaining quietly:

"The umpire didn't beat us—Baltimore did it by putting three over the fence. Carbo told me Hendricks never tagged him with his glove hand and had the ball in the other hand. Carbo said Hendricks tagged Burkhart.

"I thought Burkhart was falling and couldn't see the play. I asked Burkhart: 'did you see him tag him?' Burkhart said: 'Yes, I saw him tag him.' I have to take the man's word for it."

The Reds also got off fast in this one, collecting three runs on a run-producing single by catcher Johnny Bench in the first inning and Lee May's two-run homer in the third.

But then Baltimore starter Jim Palmer settled down and the Orioles displayed their own power against Cincinnati's Gray Nolan. First baseman Boog Powell, the hulking blond bomber, got two runs back with a homer in the fourth and Hendricks tied it with a homer in the fifth.

That set the stage for the heroics by Robinson, who also made a sensational fielding play in the sixth inning as the Orioles took a 1-0 lead in the opener of this best of-7 series.

Robinson, who entered the season considered by many too old after two lackluster seasons, flashed his fielding skill at the start of the sixth inning when he took a hit away from May, eventually saving a run that could have been driven in when Helms singled later in the inning. Then the disputed call by Burkhart helped the Orioles keep alive a season-ending winning streak that now stretches to 15 victories.

And so, when Robinson came to bat in the seventh it was still 3-3 and the Orioles who had won their last 11 regular season games and three playoff games against Minnesota, needed a run. Robinson got it on a 0-1 pitch, golfing a Nolan serve over the left field fence for his homer.

Palmer, a 6-foot-3, 196-pound righthander, got off to a shaky start but shared the first game heroics with Robinson as he pitched five-hit ball before being relieved by Pete Richert with two out in the ninth.

But before the young righthander, who will be 25 next Thursday, settled down, the Reds had struck for the three runs.

The Reds opened up in the first inning with one out when Bobby Tolan lined a 1-2 pitch to right center field for a double. Tolan cruised into third when Tony Perez flied deep to right. Johnny Bench, the No. 1 bomber in the Cincinnati arsenal, then lined the next pitch to left field for a single that brought Tolan home.

Tolan got things started for the Reds again in the third when he led off by drawing a walk on a 3-2 pitch. He stole second and two outs later rode home when May tagged an 0-2 pitch over the left field fence just inside the foul line.

Suddenly, however, the momentum seemed to shift—and it was the Orioles tagging Nolan.

Paul Blair, the slender center fielder, started it for Baltimore by beating out a roller down the third base line with one out in the fourth inning for the Orioles' first hit.

Powell then lugged his over 250-pound frame to the plate and sliced a 2-0 pitch to the opposite field. The ball carried over the left field fence for a home run.

Hendricks, who weighs almost 100 pounds less than Powell, then tied it in the fifth inning by drilling Nolan's first pitch over the right field fence for his homer.

HORNS CRUNCH OU WISHBONE

Errors Offset Sooners' Bid In 41-9 Loss

By BILL CONNORS
World Sports Editor

DALLAS — Oklahoma threw Texas' own weapons at the Longhorns Saturday. The weapons were a secretly-installed version of the Wishbone formation, two paralyzing punts, a record 50-yard field goal and a fiery defense.

But the weapon the Sooners needed to win was the H-Bomb. They were out-classed, 41-9.

More practically, the Sooners needed an offense that produced for themselves, not Texas. OU scored one touchdown and gave Texas four in an inept, erring performance that wasted all the Sooners' enterprise and effort.

THE STATISTICS

	Texas	OU
First Downs	17	14
Rushing Yardage	310	212
Passing Yardage	25	10
Return Yardage	29	69
Passes	3-7-0	3-11-2
Punts	6-34.5	4-44.5
Fumbles Lost	3	4
Yards Penalized	53	7

FOR MUCH OF THE FIRST half, the sellout throng of 72,032 in the Cotton Bowl and national television audience saw the 18-point underdog Sooners make their annual embattled charge at the Longhorns.

With a parlay of stratgey and sensational kicking, the Sooners led, 3-0, until late in the second quarter. Then they gave the game away during a horrid 12-minute stretch spanning the end of the first half and the start of the second half.

That is when they lost two of their four fumbles and one of their two pass interceptions. In those 12 minutes, Texas scored four touchdowns. Three of them came on drives of 14, 21 and 25 yards, following Sooner mistakes.

With that kind of field position, Texas' thundering runners were unstoppable. They quickly wired a 14-3 lead, then widened it to 27-3 in the opening five minutes of the second half.

THE REST OF THE BEAUTIFUL afternoon was a suffering ordeal for the Sooners, who wound up with their worst defeat in this flaming rivalry since 1941, when they were beaten, 40-7. It was Texas' highest score of the series.

In winning for the 12th time in the last 13 years, Texas did not look like a super team. The No. 2 ranked Longhorns gained only 335 yards, or 146 less than their season average, and only 113 more than Oklahoma. Texas also lost three fumbles.

Worse, the Steers lost All-America split end Cotton Speyrer, who suffered a broken arm when he collided with OU safety John Shelley, while trying to catch a pass in the third quarter.

Texas needed a roughing-the-kicker penalty against Shelley

—World Staff Photo by Johnny Walker
OU quarterback Jack Mildren gives limp-leg to Texas tacklers on one of many times he carried ball.

Louisville Stuns Hurricane, 14-8

By DEAN CLARK
World Sports Writer

LOUISVILLE, Ky. — Louisville's restructured offense generated a pair of contrasting second-quarter touchdown passes and the Cardinals shattered Tulsa's Missouri Valley title hopes, 14-8, Saturday before 9,453 Homecoming fans in Fairgrounds Stadium.

Louisville struck twice within nine minutes, gaining paydirt on a four-yard flip from Gary Inman to Cookie Brinkman and a 70-yard stunner from John Madeya to Larry Hart.

Roger Gruneisen added both extra points, but his two missed field goals in the fourth quarter kept Tulsa alive until the last play of the game.

THE CARDINALS, WHO HAD averaged 25 passes per game in their first four contests, hurled only nine against the Hurricane.

But, they achieved near maximum efficiency with six completions for 134 yards and both scores. The net yardage was 27 more than Tulsa could pick up on twice as many completions.

The limited air attack was made possible by a desperate midweek shift of defensive back Greg Campbell to tailback.

Campbell, alternating explosive counter plays with the power running of fullback Bill Gatti, plowed through the Hurricane defense for 146 yards on 25 carries.

Included was a 54-yard sprint late in the fourth quarter which denied Tulsa desperately needed field position after reserve quarterback Johnny Dobbs finally ignited the Hurricane's stumbling offense.

THE STATISTICS

	Tulsa	Louis.
First downs	23	16
Rushing yardage	156	218
Passing yardage	107	134
Return yardage	21	43
Passes	12-12-2	6-9-2
Punts	6-43.8	4-44.0
Fumbles lost	3	0
Yards penalized	65	74

GATTI SLAMMED FOR 87 yards in 18 tries, boosting the Cardinals' ground total to 218—double Louisville's season overland average.

A hard-charging Louisville defense, paced by defensive tackles Horace Jones and Larry Ball and middle linebacker Amos Martin, contained Tulsa well inside its own territory until Dobbs replaced sophomore Drew Pearson with 3:31 left in the third period.

A vital weapon in Louisville's field position supremacy was the 44-yard punting average of Scott Marcus, 10 yards above his season mark.

Marcus climaxed his day of booming punts with a pressurized 48-yarder that died on Tulsa's 11-yard line with just 49 seconds to play.

A 10-YARD PASS FROM Dobbs to Johnny White and a long holding penalty moved the ball to the Louisville 47 with 15 seconds remaining.

But Ball and Jones, the only two rushers in Louisville's prevent defense, sliced through Tulsa's line and dropped Dobbs before he could get off one last attempt.

A midfield fumble by Josh Ashton on Tulsa's second offensive play of the game put

Continued on S-8

Tulsa	0	0	0	8	— 8
Louisville	0	14	0	0	— 14

L—Brinkman 4 pass from Inman (Gruneisen kick)
L—Hart 70 pass from Madeya (Gruneisen kick)
T—Dobbs 1 run (E. White pass from

OSU DEFENSE SKINS FROGS, 34-20

By TOM LOBAUGH
World Sports Writer

STILLWATER — Oklahoma State's hard-nosed defense held Texas Christian at bay for two periods, and also set up the scoring opportunities as the Cowboys moved to a 34-20 victory in their non-conference football game before 24,500 fans at Lewis Stadium Saturday.

Three fumble recoveries and

THE STATISTICS

	TCU	OSU
First downs	13	17
Rushing yardage	201	174
Passing yardage	71	199
Return yardage	98	[illegible]

66-yard punt to the Frog five. But the kicking game put the Cowboys in trouble in the second half.

One blocked punt, and one partially-blocked, set up the first two TCU tallies. And Danny Colbert raced 89 yards for another TD after taking Benien's booming 46-yard kick in the final period.

But the Cowboys had put the game out of reach before the belated Frog rally. OSU had a 17-0 halftime advantage, and it was 31-7 before the visitors tallied twice in the fourth quarter.

Fullback James Williams scored the first OSU touchdown on a 12-yard plunge midway of the second period, after Lee Stover had intercepted at the TCU 15.

Soccer-style kicker Uwe Pruss, who converted the first TD, added a 41-yard field goal, but injured his right ankle on the play, and was unable to return.

Getting the ball on John Carter's fumble recovery at midfield with only 49 seconds left in the half, Pounds engineered a five-play scoring drive before the gun. He passed the Pokes to the one, then sneaked for six points, and Pat Clapp added the extra point.

Larry Harris, former Northeastern A&M halfback, scored over the middle from a yard out for TCU's first touchdown, early in the third quarter. The tally was set up when Benien's punt was blocked by Frog tackle Ken Steel, and covered by cornerbacker Gary Webb at the Cowboy six.

Pounds proceeded to move the Cowboys far in front by tossing TD passes of 30 yards to Bobby Cole and eight yards to Tom Dearinger before the third quarter ended, with Clapp coming through with the extra points.

TCU'S LAST TWO TALLIES came in a two-minute span midway of the last period. Steel partially blocked Benien's punt at the 50, and the Frogs moved to score, with Raymond Thodes

Hogs Buffalo Bears, 41-7

In 1970, OU coaches decided to switch from the veer to the wishbone offense. A bye week before the Texas game was used to hastily install the new offense. The results were disastrous. OU suffered five turnovers, losing to Texas 41-9. The following week, OU upset 13th-ranked Colorado.

our way.' And he said, 'Yeah, you are on your way back to Arkansas.' "

OU upset 13th-ranked Colorado the following week, but got booed in a home loss to Kansas State. Coaches perhaps were a sliver away from being fired when Iowa State jumped to a 21-0 first-quarter lead in the seventh game of the season. The Sooners rallied for a 29-28 victory, getting the winning points on Pruitt's two-point conversion run with 2:24 left.

Before that comeback, OU had lost seven of its past 14 games. From that game through the next five seasons, the Sooners went 58-4-2. Former offensive lineman Terry Webb said the wishbone was the key.

"We did it unlike anybody else had ever done it before," he said. "People had never seen that kind of speed out of the wishbone. It had been more of a power game, the way Alabama and Texas had been running it."

Fairbanks told the Tulsa World in 1972 that OU assistants did not sleep much or see much of their families when they rushed to install the wishbone in 1970. Coaches had to learn the offense before they could relay the blueprint to players.

> "There was a guy that was a federal judge named Frank Seay from Seminole and he called me after the Texas game and said, 'Are you crazy?' I said, 'Frank, we are on our way.' And he said, 'Yeah, you are on your way back to Arkansas.' "
>
> — *Larry Lacewell*

"Barry Switzer is the hardest-working sonofagun I've ever seen," Lacewell told the Tulsa World. "That poor guy must have worn out half a dozen projectors studying film. He had to do it all the hard way and he did a great job of teaching our kids."

OU's success with the wishbone made Switzer one of the nation's hottest head coaching prospects.

He didn't have to leave town to get a job.

After handing off the ball, University of Oklahoma quarterback Jack Mildren (11) watches Joe Wylie (22) go over Texas' David Richardson (34) in a 1970 game. The game, OU's first running the wishbone, ended in a 41-9 Texas victory.

CHAPTER 5

Head coach and high times

"We were young country boys that thought we knew it all and we had the best ideas and the best players and the best recruiting coaches. ... We wanted to beat them all. And we didn't mind telling everybody we were great."

— *Larry Lacewell*

In 1973, Switzer's first season as head coach, the Sooners went 10-0-1. The team tied the University of Southern California 7-7 in Switzer's second game. He is pictured during his first home game — against the University of Miami — as head coach. OU won, 24-20.

PULLING THE RIGHT STRINGS

Barry Switzer is shown on the OU football field in Norman with his wife, Kay, and three children after being named head coach in 1973. Switzer is holding his son Doug, while Kathy and Greg are standing in the front. His first-year salary was $24,000.

Barry Switzer was named Oklahoma's head football coach on Jan. 29, 1973. He would later be called "The King" by people in the state. The nickname, according to The Oklahoman's Berry Tramel, was birthed by former OU sports information department staffers Larry McAlister and Pat Hanlon and caught fire after being popularized by Oklahoma City sports radio icon Al Eschbach.

Two things:

1. Switzer doesn't like the nickname. "It always embarrassed me," he told the Tulsa World in 2009.

2. The King's first crown was a black hat.

No sooner had Switzer been promoted than it was learned OU would be placed on a two-year probation because transcripts had been altered for two freshmen the previous year.

Offensive line coach Bill Michael was the fall-on-the-sword figure in the ordeal.

"Frankly, Bill Michael bit the bullet for the entire coaching staff," former assistant coach Larry Lacewell said. Michael, who played side by side with Switzer at

Darrell Royal and Barry Switzer are shown during the OU-Texas game in 1975. A year later, the Red River Rivalry heated up when Texas coach Royal accused OU of spying on his team's practices and offered $10,000 each to Switzer, defensive coordinator Larry Lacewell and the man he accused of spying if they would take polygraph tests. They declined. Royal retired after the 1976 season.

Arkansas, was forced to resign.

The fallout from the altered transcript was no TV, no bowl games and a perception that OU was a rogue program. Switzer responded with fire, saying that the punishers made a mistake because they didn't ban the Sooners from pursuing a Big Eight title and a national championship.

Said former offensive lineman Terry Webb, "He used a little more colorful language, but Barry would basically have meetings with us and would tell us stuff like, 'They can take away this and take away that, but they didn't tell us that we couldn't go out and kick their asses.' And he started this from day one and said that's exactly what we are going to do. We are going to become the best team that nobody ever saw."

Switzer fired up the masses by saying similar things at booster functions and would add comments in the same vein, claiming that he is double parked and had better move his car before being penalized for that, too. He once told a booster group in Tulsa that, whatever had gone on, he didn't have a damn thing to do with Watergate in 1972.

Switzer was a master of spinning situations to his advantage.

"If there was ever a perfect situation for the right person at the right time at the right place, that was it," Webb said.

Playing the us-against-the-world card had the desired effect. The Sooners didn't experience defeat until Switzer's 31st game as head coach.

In between, Switzer's reputation as a brash pup (he got the OU job at age 35) was ratcheted up when he feuded with Texas

> "If there was ever a perfect situation for the right person at the right time at the right place, that was it."
>
> — *Terry Webb, former OU offensive lineman*

coach Darrell Royal, who, truth in name, was college football royalty.

"We were young and we opened our mouths too much – way too much," Lacewell said. "We shot our mouths off. We wanted it all. We were young country boys that thought we knew it all and we had the best ideas and the best players and the best recruiting coaches. ... We wanted to beat them all. And we didn't mind telling everybody we were great."

While the coaches were engaged in the Red River Rivalry, Royal accused the Switzer regime of spying and cheating. Smoke? Fire? And Switzer believed Royal was behind the football coaches association's moves to ban the honoring of coaches whose teams were on probation and to make teams on probation ineligible for inclusion in the coaches poll. Switzer responded by saying he thought such things only occurred in Russia.

Texas coach Darrell Royal, shown with Barry Switzer in 1975, took offense at remarks made by Switzer to an alumni group that were quoted in the Tulsa World.

"The world assumes that OU cheats," Lacewell said. "The word 'Sooner' – if you remember – those were the people who broke across the line the earliest (at the Oklahoma Land Run). But it was the state of Texas which really pinned the black hat on us because we were beating their favorite team. (And) we didn't know how to shut up."

The most attention-getting example came when Royal and Switzer had opposite opinions about possible cost-cutting legislation in 1975. Switzer was speaking to an alumni group in Tulsa and said some coaches "don't want to coach any more. They would rather sit home and listen to guitar pickers. They want to make it to where you can't outwork anybody."

> "I wasn't mature enough (when I made the guitar picker comment). That's one of those things I do regret."
>
> — Barry Switzer

Royal got steamed when those words appeared in print and called Tulsa World sports editor Bill Connors with a salty response.

"I didn't know Bill was going to write that," Switzer recalled decades later. "But it was true and the thing about it was ... I didn't realize how (Texas) people were saying the same thing. He was hearing that already down there from people (and was) sensitive or paranoid about what his people thought."

Royal was 50 at the time. He retired after the 1976 season.

Switzer's 70th birthday was approaching when he said this in 2007: "Hell, I would rather listen to guitar pickers, too. By the time I was 50, I would damn sure rather have been doing what he was doing instead of chasing high school football players, 17- and 18-year-old kids. So I understood (later). I wasn't mature enough (when I made the guitar picker comment). That's one of those things I do regret."

Switzer described himself as "just a boy from south Arkansas" before becoming a head coach. But as Connors wrote in 1973: "His fast, no-drawl speech, stylishly sporty wardrobe and handsome features make him look and sound more like a thinning,

Oklahoma coach Barry Switzer is carried off the field by his Sooners after defeating Michigan in the Orange Bowl in 1976.

blond-haired Californian who might be modeling alpaca sweaters with Frank Gifford."

Switzer was eager, but not jumpy, to be a head coach. His mentor, Jim Mackenzie, believed a coach should consider getting out of the profession if he reached age 35 and he wasn't yet a head coach.

> "His fast, no-drawl speech, stylishly sporty wardrobe and handsome features make him look and sound more like a thinning, blond-haired Californian who might be modeling alpaca sweaters with Frank Gifford."
>
> — *Bill Connors, Tulsa World sports editor, of Switzer*

Before being named OU's head coach, Switzer was offered the Iowa State job, interviewed at Michigan State, Rice and SMU and was contacted by representatives from other schools, including Colorado.

"I have three or four more years ahead of me before I need to make a move," Switzer said in a 1968 Oklahoman story about his desire to be a head coach. "Right now I feel my future remains in Norman."

Emotionally, Switzer had been on a roller coaster when he got his big break. His third child was born in September 1972. His father died in November. The Michigan State flirtation came in December. And, in January 1973, Chuck Fairbanks pulled Switzer aside to say he was leaving OU to take an NFL job.

"Chuck wanted me to go with him," Switzer recalled in 2007. "He wanted me to be his backfield coach with the New England Patriots. I said, 'Hell, I would rather have this job.' He said, 'I know that, but if you don't (get it), I want you to come with me.' Three days passed and (OU regent) Jack Santee got them all settled down. They made the right decision."

Those three days felt like forever to Switzer and the players he would inherit.

"It was interesting times for us," Webb said. "The word we had all gotten was they were going to go outside of the staff for a

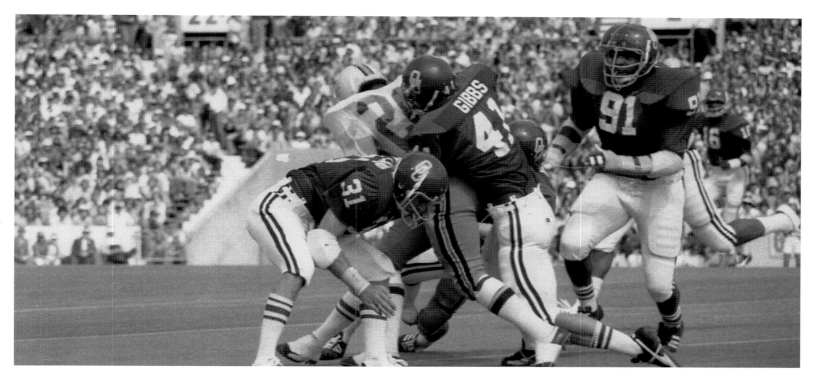

OU's Gary Gibbs (41) tackles a Wake Forest player during the Sooners' 63-0 victory on Oct. 5, 1974. Gibbs collected signatures for a petition in support of Switzer as the successor to Chuck Fairbanks, who departed to join the NFL as coach of the New England Patriots. Gibbs later succeeded Switzer and coached OU from 1989-94.

'name.' We were all real concerned about that at that time. (Linebacker) Gary Gibbs – GG we used to call him – he kind of got a petition up and had gotten all the players to sign it, saying that we wanted – and the assistants wanted – Barry to be the guy. Now, how much influence that had on their decision, I have no way of really knowing."

Webb said Gibbs' petition got "total support" from players because the Sooners had been successful and nobody wanted to

Barry Switzer and others enjoy drinks at Pat O'Brien's, a bar in New Orleans, before the 1972 Sugar Bowl game. Pictured (from left) are: Dale Boutwell, Switzer, and OU assistant coaches Larry Lacewell and Jerry Pettibone.

start over with a new staff and a new system.

Assistant coach Larry Lacewell called it probably the most unique situation in the history of coaching searches because "nobody else here even wanted the job, and that's got to be a first. Everybody just knew it had to be Barry and wanted him to have it."

Why? "Well, I think it was because of his people skills," Michael said. "He was smart and had great people skills. He could get along with anybody. It didn't matter who you were or where you came from and we all knew his background, who he was and where he came from. So it was a natural, easy transition there. There wasn't any doubt in my mind that they picked the right guy."

Switzer was hired at a first-year salary of $24,000. Michael never got to coach a game under Switzer because it was determined Michael had knowledge of the altered transcripts which landed the Sooners on probation. Lacewell said letting Michael go was "probably one of the most severe things Barry has had to do in his life."

If you think a parting of ways negatively impacted the relationship between Michael and Switzer, you're mistaken.

"Life takes a lot of twists and turns, but there is one thing it can't take away and that's die-hard friendships and that's what we have," Michael said, indicating that his years at OU were "the best" and he still enjoys spending time with Switzer.

Michael, who resides in Corinth, Texas, was looking at a game ball in his living room as he was being interviewed for this book. The ball, stored in a bookcase, means something to him.

OU hammered Texas 52-13 in Switzer's fourth game as head coach. Afterward, players who were fond of Michael wanted Switzer to give a game ball to the departed coach. (Michael said it was Joe Washington's idea.)

Michael was presented the ball in what was intended to be a discreet ceremony a few days later. Even in a pre-Internet age, secrets were hard to keep. When news hit print that OU had given a game ball to a jettisoned assistant, Switzer's hat got blacker.

Michael was humbled and appreciative that he was given a game ball. Ask him if Switzer deserves a black hat.

Said Michael, "To me, he is one of the better people I have ever known."

From an X's and O's standpoint, "Transcriptgate" seemed costly because it caused quarterback Kerry Jackson, who understudied behind Dave Robertson in 1972, to be declared ineligible in 1973.

That meant Switzer was forced to begin his head coaching career with raw prospects Steve Davis, Scott Hill and Joe McReyn-

"I had a TV show. I was the only assistant coach in the country that had one and it came on an hour before (ABC's college football game) every Saturday. ... Everybody knew me. I had a Cadillac and an Oldsmobile. I turned down being the head coach at Iowa. I turned down Kansas State. OU was the highest of all of them. It never got any better."

— *Larry Lacewell*

olds at quarterback. Davis went 32-1-1 the next three seasons as the wishbone went sweeping down the plains.

From Switzer's last seven games as an OU assistant through his early years as a head coach, the Sooners went 37 consecutive games without tasting defeat. The only blemish was a tie against USC in 1973.

Oklahoma didn't lose a game in 1973 or 1974. The Sooners won national championships in 1974 and 1975. The wishbone assault spawned big, bold headlines and OU's defenses were farm clubs for NFL franchises.

"We were just demolishing teams," Lacewell said, crediting "damn good" coaches and excellent players.

Keep in mind that, long before Switzer replaced Fairbanks, he said this: "I don't know if I could ever be a head coach because assistant coaches have more fun."

The promotion did not prove to be an obstacle to fun.

"We had a great time," Lacewell said.

The coaching staff was full of characters and Lacewell – a defensive whiz whose other skill was making people laugh – was front and center.

"I had a TV show," he said. "I was the only assistant coach in the country that had one and it came on an hour before (ABC's college football game) every Saturday. ... Everybody knew me. I had a Cadillac and an Oldsmobile. I turned down being the head coach at Iowa. I turned down Kansas State. OU was the highest of all of them. It never got any better."

Lacewell was asked if celebrities hung around the football program during that era. He recalled escorting Cincinnati Reds slugger Johnny Bench into the dressing room to meet players. But, after giving the question some thought, Lacewell said this:

"We were the famous people."

Wins were enjoyed – and they were shared with as many people as could squeeze into Switzer's house. Lacewell said parties

TULSA SUNDAY WORLD

72nd Year—No. 27   *Final Home Edition*   Tulsa, Oklahoma, Sunday, October 10, 1976   *Single Copy—35c*   211 Pages—16 Parts

Ford Signs Beef Quota On Imports

DALLAS (UPI)— Just one day after promising Midwest cattlemen affirmative action to deal with declining domestic meat prices, President Ford imposed a quota Saturday to limit foreign beef imports to the United States this year.

It was an action Democrat Jimmy Carter had earlier claimed was overdue.

Ford, in a proclamation signed aboard Air Force One during a flight to Texas from Lawton, set a beef import ceiling at 1.23 billion pounds.

The President's new limit fell about 17 million pounds below the import

Related News On A-22

levels the Agriculture Department had projected earlier for 1976.

Ford's action was based on the 1964 meat import quota act, which was passed to give the President authority to protect domestic prices based on quarterly estimates supplied by the Agriculture department.

IN HIS PROCLAMATION, FORD said the quota "is required by overriding economic interests of the United States."

U. S. cattlemen have sought the quotas for several weeks, citing a drop in prices for domestic meat.

Kansas, Texas and Oklahoma cattlemen met privately with Ford in Lawton Friday, pressing for some indication whether he would aid them. After the meeting, White House officials quoted the President as saying there was a "high degree of likelihood of affirmative action."

Acting Secretary of Agriculture John A. Knebel said imported beef usually

barred all meat imports and Japan has imposed a one-year cutoff.

Campaigning Friday in El Paso, Tex., Carter called on Ford to impose the quotas since, for the last three years, cattle producers have been losing $50 to $100 on each animal they sell.

Consumers, too, will suffer in the long run if the present conditions are allowed to continue. As fewer and fewer cattle are raised for market, beef prices may once again skyrocket to their 1973 levels, Carter said.

Storm Dumps Heavy Rain on Eastern States

Floods, Tornados Cause Damage, 4 Persons Killed

United Press International

An autumn storm system laced with tornados Saturday dumped up to eight inches of rain along the Atlantic Coast from South Carolina into southern New England, with many rivers and streams raging out of their banks.

Six tornados were reported in North

Escorts for the President
University of Oklahoma football coach Barry Switzer, left, and Darrell Royal, football coach at the University of Texas, escort President Ford on the field at the Cotton Bowl in Dallas Saturday.   Ford attended the traditional game between the two rivals during his visit here.

'OU Spy' T-Shirts for Sale

Royal's Charges Provide Lighter Note for Shootout

OSU Upsets Kansas; OU Ties Texas

The Tulsa World front page on Oct. 10, 1976, includes a photo of Switzer with President Gerald Ford and Texas football coach Darrell Royal. The story details Royal's allegations against OU of spying on his team. President Ford attended the OU-Texas game and was escorted onto the field by the two coaches. "OU Spy" T-shirts were on sale at the game, the story said. The game ended in a 6-6 tie.

after games were "all-night affairs. Nobody celebrated victory more than we did."

Jim Riley, who played for OU in the 1960s, and Billy Gilbow, Switzer's roommate at Arkansas, used Switzer's tickets at home games and afterward would go to the coach's house to "sit and drink and holler and scream and act stupid."

Riley said Switzer invited old friends from all over the country to attend the parties. Reporters showed up because Riley said Switzer had nothing to hide. That doesn't mean everything that happened there was printable.

"One time we all spent a little time in the pool together with our clothes on," Riley said. "We just started pushing everybody in the pool. We decided that was funny. Switzer would come up to me or I came up to him and he said, 'You are not going to do this.' And I said, 'Oh yes we are.' I grabbed his little ass and ... I just dove in with him."

> "We never wanted to go to bed. We stayed up to three or four or five in the morning. I (filled in on) his (playback) show a lot. He couldn't make it. He had the 'flu.' "
>
> — *Larry Lacewell*

Lacewell said he and Switzer would usually be among the last people standing at the bashes.

"We never wanted to go to bed," Lacewell said. "We stayed up to three or four or five in the morning. I (filled in on) his (playback) show a lot. He couldn't make it. He had the 'flu.' "

Victors deserve to have a good time but Lacewell said, "We probably abused it a little bit. We were kids. We weren't 45-year-old coaches. We were 35, 34, 36 from Crossett, Ark., and Fordyce, Ark. I wasn't a big-shot Division I player. I was thrilled to death to be a big shot and I think Barry Switzer was too."

A party pooper arrived on Nov. 8, 1975.

Kansas' Nolan Cromwell is tackled by Oklahoma's Dewey Selmon (91) during OU's game with Kansas on Nov. 8, 1975. Also pictured is OU player Daryl Hunt (85). Kansas won, 23-3, ending OU's 28-game winning streak.

Switzer (center) poses with quarterback Steve Davis (left) and running back Joe Washing-ton as they signal "No. 1" in Miami Beach, Fla., on Jan. 2, 1976. The Associated Press had just named the Sooners the national champions for the second year in a row.

Oklahoma had won 28 consecutive games and had scored touchdowns in 99 consecutive games. Both streaks ended in a 23-3 loss to Kansas. Switzer's first loss came in his third season.

"The one thing I feared finally happened," Lacewell said. "We played bad and got beat by Kansas. I wanted to play good and get beat. But we played bad and got beat by a damn good team. They were good. They beat us in Norman. It broke my heart."

OU had a punt blocked before the end of the first half and followed that by committing turnovers on eight consecutive possessions. Afterward, Switzer told the press the Sooners beat themselves.

"I lost one college game," Webb said. "And it was so odd when we did lose that game, I just figured, 'Oh man, we are fixing to get our butts ripped in here. Coach is fixing to go berserk.' He had one speech, he told us. He got up. And we were all down. He said, 'Men, we rode that train for a long time. It had to come to an end some day. This was that day. Let's get back up on that train again.' That was all he said. It was amazing. He always knew the right thing to say."

Sometimes, the right thing to say was making sure players kept revelry within reason.

Rolling along unbeaten, OU had little reason to be motivated for a 1974 game against Oklahoma State. Switzer looked across the street from Owen Field for motivation. A few weeks before Bedlam, Webb said there had been a "small incident" at O'Connell's Pub, a popular player hangout.

"Guys got rowdy and a sheriff's department car showed up and the car got rocked pretty good – not rocks thrown at it, but people standing around and rocking it, actually physically rocking the car," Webb said. "They told Barry about it and the next day it was padlocked."

Switzer wielded enough clout to keep the padlock on the door for a week or more, according to Webb.

Said Webb, "At one of his meetings, Barry said, 'Men, if you all ever want that damn place to be opened up again ... here's what you should do to Oklahoma State.' Needless to say, I don't think I played the second half. And when we got back to Norman, O'Connell's was opened up and on the bar there was all kinds of food spread out."

After the loss to Kansas in 1975, the Sooners regrouped in time to salvage a national championship.

About those post-game parties: Riley said one of the things attendees talked about was, "When is Barry Switzer going to lose a game?"

Said Riley, "When he lost that game to Kansas, people were starting to grumble. You know how some OU fans are. They would grumble, 'I warned you guys when you hired him that, sooner or later, he would lose a game, and sure enough he has. My God, let's run his ass off.' When Barry heard that, he loved it."

Lacewell recalled lying on the floor with partiers at Switzer's home yelling "too much ain't never enough, too much ain't never enough."

Said Lacewell, "We wanted it all."

Switzer's '70s show was more successful than "That '70s Show." His record as a head coach during the 1970s was 73-7-2.

"It was just great times," Webb said. "The times were so good that I remember when Rex Norris came on with our staff and he would tell us sometimes, 'Men, I know you all don't understand, but it doesn't happen like this all the time.' Me and the guys I came up with, we thought this was the way it was. ... We were just dumb-ass country boys. We were playing because we enjoyed playing and we happened to be good at it. We didn't realize what kind of history we were making."

Oklahoma head coach Barry Switzer, shown with Elvis Peacock (4) and other players, enjoys the closing moments of a game against Nebraska in Norman on Nov. 25, 1977. The Sooners won, 38-7.

CHAPTER 6

Pearl beer

"The thing was, if I got over 100 yards in a football game, I would get a chicken fried steak. I still hold the (Texas state) record — 38 straight games with (at least) 100 yards. They thought I was running for the record. I was running for that chicken fried damn steak."

— *Billy Sims*

Billy Sims moved to Hooks, Texas, to live with his grandparents and discovered that everyone in Texas plays football. He started playing in 10th grade and racked up 7,738 yards during his high school career.

THE CLASS OF RECRUITING

The urban legend: Before stepping inside the Killeen, Texas, home of recruit Frank Blevins in the 1980s, Barry Switzer rummaged through a garbage can outside and saw empty cans of Pearl beer.

Later, when Blevins' father asked Switzer if he would like a beer, the coach is alleged to have said, "Only if it's Pearl beer, because that's the only kind I drink."

Why sift through a trash can to gain an edge in recruiting? Because no coach wins big over the long haul with average players. Or, to paraphrase Switzer's friend and former Oklahoma State basketball coach Eddie Sutton, a jackass has never won the Kentucky Derby. Switzer populated his teams with Thoroughbreds.

"There are too many good coaches who are products of good systems," Switzer once told the Tulsa World. "I am no better and no worse than anybody else. Players win and players lose."

Switzer indicated he was fortunate to work at a tradition-rich institution that appealed to the best players and assistant coaches.

"Player acquisition is the thing and the good players at Oklahoma did not just fall out of the sky," he said. "I have a lot to do with recruiting. I enjoy selling our program. I think I am good at it."

That's an understatement.

Said former player Greg Roberts: "He's a hell of a salesman."

Roberts, an Outland Trophy recipient in 1978, was part of an epic OU recruiting class in 1975. There were 19 players on the Dallas Times-Herald's Texas blue-chip list that year and 13 signed with the Sooners. If that had happened in the Scout and

Billy Sims spent his childhood years in St. Louis, Mo., where inner city kids played baseball and their heroes were Cardinals players such as Bob Gibson. "We didn't even think about football," Sims said.

Rivals era, the Internet would have gone supernova.

Running back Kenny King of Clarendon, Texas, was in "the" class. His father wanted him to go to Texas A&M. He signed with OU. Then he played in a Texas high school all-star game in Fort Worth and shared a field with the likes of Roberts, Thomas Lott, Billy Sims, George Cumby, Bud Hebert, Phil Tabor, Paul Tabor and Uwe von Schamann.

King couldn't help but notice the obvious.

"All of these guys are now going to the University of Oklahoma," he said. "I made the right choice."

Switzer made a living out of cherry-picking Texas and bringing back "converts" to the Oklahoma side of the Red River.

Said former player Jim Riley, "Somebody once asked me did I ever want to go into college coaching. And I said, 'Hell, no.' You have to kiss the butts of those 16-year-old and 17-year-old (recruits)? No, thank you. I ain't doing that. But Barry had a way with them. They just fell in love with him, all of them."

> "... [P]eople came there to play for Barry. They didn't come to play for the University of Oklahoma. ... You would have run through a wall for the man."
>
> — *Terry Webb, former OU offensive lineman*

Marcus Dupree was such a superstar high school player that a book was written about his recruitment. Dupree loved hearing Switzer talk about hanging half a hundred points on opponents.

And Switzer's background permitted him to be a chameleon. Drop him in any environment and ...

"He just blends in," Roberts said. "He's just one of the guys. You feel comfortable around him."

Switzer pulled out all the stops in pursuing Sims. Switzer dispatched assistant coach Bill Shimek to stake out Sims in

Hooks, Texas. Sims said Shimek spent 77 days in Hooks and was made an honorary citizen.

"We were like a pro team," former assistant coach Larry Lacewell said. "We stuck a couple of guys out on the road in the fall almost full-time."

Sims spent childhood years in St. Louis. He said inner city kids played baseball ("We didn't even think about football") at that time and St. Louis Cardinals players such as Bob Gibson were his heroes.

J.C. Watts hands the ball off to Billy Sims during OU's game with Nebraska on Nov. 24, 1979.

When Sims moved to Hooks to live with grandparents, he discovered everyone in Texas plays football.

"So I didn't really start playing football until I was in the 10th grade," he said. "I started off as a linebacker. I saw this guy running with the ball and 11 guys were trying to kill him. I said, 'That can't be fun.' So I played linebacker and I was third-string running back."

Players would refer to Barry Switzer as OU's first black coach, according to former offensive lineman Terry Webb. "I can't think of any better way to put it. If you know him, you know what I'm talking about. If you don't, you never will."

Then the first- and second-string running backs (one was Sims' cousin) got hurt. Welcome to the first team.

"I was scared," Sims said. "I thought about that guy with the ball (getting killed) so I just made people miss and I got pretty good at it and the rest is history."

Sims dodged enough tacklers to rush for 7,738 yards during his high school career.

"The thing was, if I got over 100 yards in a football game, I would get a chicken fried steak," he said. "I still hold the (Texas state) record – 38 straight games with (at least) 100 yards. They thought I was running for the record. I was running for that chicken fried damn steak."

Problem for Switzer: Sims seemed bound for Baylor. It was a Baptist school. Sims came from a Baptist family. His grandmother loved Baylor coach Grant Teaff. Sims wanted to make her happy.

Sims said his high school baseball coach was from Durant and talked him into taking a recruiting visit to Oklahoma, even though he was committed to Baylor.

"I met Bud Wilkinson and I met Greg Pruitt and I saw Joe Washington and Steve Davis and Tinker Owens and the Selmon brothers and all these guys," Sims said. "And I didn't realize they had all these Texas players on the team – some of them I knew about in high school – because they were on probation. Nobody saw them on TV."

During the trip to Norman, Switzer made this pitch: "Hey, I know you're going to Baylor, but, before you leave, I want you

> "... [T]hey took me to a club ... there were Indian players, there were white players, there were Hispanic players, there were black players. I said right then and there that if they party together off the field, they will play like champions on the field ..."
>
> — *Kenny King, former OU running back*

"He says, 'Kenny King, take the wheel, take the wheel.' I said, 'I'm not touching that wheel.' And the pilot is like, 'No, no, you will be fine. We're not going to die.' So I take the wheel and all of a sudden we are doing this little dip and I'm like 'Oh God, we're going to die.' "

— *Kenny King, former OU running back*

to meet my family."

Sure. What harm can come of that?

When Sims arrived at Switzer's house, all three of the coach's children were wearing No. 20 jerseys. Switzer told Sims they were already selling his jerseys in Norman.

"Wow! Really coach?" Sims said, not knowing any better. "Then they all turn around and they have got 'Sims' on the back of the jerseys. That was impressive."

While Sims was tearing up east Texas, King was a small-town whiz in west Texas. King said he got discovered in Clarendon because a sports writer publicized his exploits in the Amarillo newspaper.

Switzer flew to Clarendon on a small airplane to pick up King and they flew to Norman together.

"It was the first time I had ever been in a plane and now I'm in this little two-engine thing and I don't know what the heck I'm doing up there," King said.

"I'm in the co-pilot seat and coach Switzer is back there and he is talking. You know how coach gets to going when he is talking. He says, 'Kenny King, take the wheel, take the wheel.' I said, 'I'm not touching that wheel.' And the pilot is like, 'No, no, you will be fine. We're not going to die.' So I take the wheel and all of a sudden we are doing this little dip and I'm like 'Oh God, we're going to die.' "

King, of course, survived the trip and, during a visit to Switzer's office, was wowed by

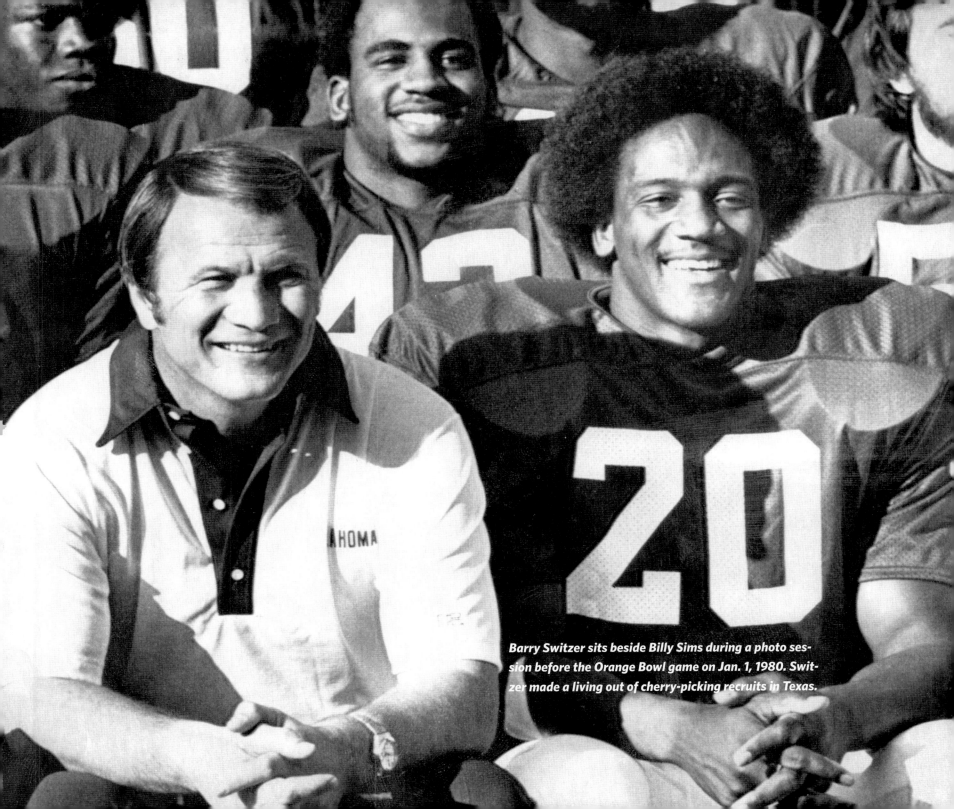

Barry Switzer sits beside Billy Sims during a photo session before the Orange Bowl game on Jan. 1, 1980. Switzer made a living out of cherry-picking recruits in Texas.

"Player acquisition is the thing and the good players at Oklahoma did not just fall out of the sky. I have a lot to do with recruiting. I enjoy selling our program. I think I am good at it."

— *Barry Switzer*

a tradition-thick sales pitch. Then came a "horrible" visit to Texas and King became more convinced that OU was the place for him.

Leaving nothing to chance, Switzer stayed at the Western Skies Hotel in Clarendon the night before signing day and went to the pool hall to shoot pool with the locals. Maybe the townsfolk were awed by a big-time coach showing up at the pool hall, but the fact of the matter is he was back in his natural habitat, like Crossett all over again.

"To have the head coach at the University of Oklahoma come to Clarendon, Texas, and spend the night to sign me, I felt like I was important," King said.

King said he was looking for two things in a school. He wanted an opportunity to "just fit into an organization." And he was looking for a non-prejudiced environment. He said a majority of his friends in high school were white, but he had seen enough racism to know he wanted to get away from it.

"When I went to Oklahoma, they took me to a club called the Blue Onion or something," King said. "And when I walked in, there were Indian players, there were white players, there were Hispanic players, there were black players. I said right then and there that if they party together off the field, they will play like champions on the field together and that's exactly what it was like."

Those close to Switzer will tell you he is not given enough credit for knocking

Thomas Lott became the first black starting quarterback at OU in 1976. Lott's trademark was a bandana that flowed out of his helmet. He is shown at the Orange Bowl with Barry Switzer on Dec. 28, 1977. The Sooners lost to Arkansas, 31-6.

down color barriers. College football was integrated by the time Switzer arrived at OU as an assistant coach, but many programs hesitated to usher in change or seemed bound by a quota system.

"His real and lasting contribution as a coach, when he became a head coach in 1973, Barry made it clear to everyone that we were going to play the best players," former coach and athletic director Donnie Duncan told the Tulsa World in 2007. "It didn't make any difference who they were or where they came from or how much money they had or their family had. The opportunities to kids who needed opportunities got them and did great things because of Barry's heart. That will be his legacy. He changed lives and futures with the kids he touched."

> "... [K]ids who needed opportunities got them and did great things because of Barry's heart. That will be his legacy. He changed lives and futures with the kids he touched."
>
> — Donnie Duncan, former OU athletic director

Some white coaches at that time had never spent meaningful time around African-Americans. Lacewell said the opposite was true at OU.

Former offensive lineman Terry Webb said players used to refer to Switzer as OU's first black head coach. Explanation? "It's just because he was just Barry," Webb said. "I can't think of any better way to put it. If you know him, you know what I'm talking about. If you don't, you never will."

Thomas Lott, one of the Texas high school recruits, became OU's first black starting quarterback in 1976. He said one of the things that blew his mind when he arrived in Norman was the number of black players.

"I thought I must have made a wrong turn and went to Grambling because there were so many of us there," he said.

Switzer allowed his recruits to be individuals. Joe Washington wore silver shoes. Lott's trademark was a bandana that flowed out of his helmet.

It Was Just Another Day- Almost

To a 'Degree', Sims Thankful for Heisman

By CLAY HENRY
World Sports Writer

NORMAN — FOR BILLY SIMS, TUESDAY, NOV. 28, 1978 was just another day at the University of Oklahoma. It meant getting up and going to Botany class. After all, earning a degree is more important than winning the Heisman Trophy.

Oklahoma's junior halfback from Hooks, Tex., did go to class Tuesday morning before accepting the Heisman Trophy in typical Billy Sims fashion.

He didn't appear any different than the cool, mature 23-year-old who had taken in stride both the good things and the bad things during a most unusual season.

He went to bed early Monday night and "slept like a baby and, no,

I didn't say any prayers. Me and the Man Upstairs have an understanding." He would have slept until just before time to go to his 9:30 Botany class, but his phone began ringing early.

"Finally, we just got up and started talking about the Heisman," said Greg Roberts, who shares suite 114 in the Bud Wilkinson Complex with Sims.

"I couldn't miss that Botany class," Sims said. "It's my toughest class. I wanted to go today because we got a test back from last week. I did pretty good. I've got a "C" average in that class."

Sims has a special reason for wanting his degree in recreational therapy for the handicap.

"My younger brother, Darrel, is 15 and he's mentally retarded.

Not by much, but he is disturbed. He can play soccer and hockey, but he doesn't play football," Sims said. "I know some kids never will be able to get the pleasure out of playing football. Someday, when I'm finished playing football, I want to go back to Hooks, maybe, and start a recreation center for handicapped kids."

Sims the only time he really felt excited Tuesday was when John Farrell of the Downtown Athletic Club telephoned to tell him he had won the Heisman.

"I think my heart stopped for a second. Then I just said, 'Thank you, I appreciate it.' I don't guess Hooks will ever be the same. I'm supposed to go down there for a Billy Sims day Saturday. They were going to have it even if I didn't win. They might make it last a whole week now," Sims said.

"This is an award for the team. Without the offensive line, I wouldn't have been up for the Heisman Trophy. Their blocking makes a running back" Sims said.

Would he give part of the Heisman to Roberts, the quick offensive guard who cleared the way for him? "He (Roberts) can have all of it," Sims laughed. "The main thing is that I believe in the Man Upstairs. I put Him before anything."

Roberts, the quick offensive guard who cleared the way for Sims, and Thomas Lott, the wishbone quarterback who made things click, stormed into the press conference in the OU Student Union after Sims had been there about 15 minutes.

"Now we've got everything," Sims said to Roberts, who Sunday picked up the Outland Trophy as the nation's premier lineman "They'll (the trophies) make nice book ends."

Sims began joking with his two best friends. "No line and no quarterback. I did everything," Sims blurted out just before nearly falling out of his chair laughing.

Roberts said all the media attention hasn't changed Sims "We've been friends for four years and he's always been the same. We've always done things together and there has never been anything wrong," Roberts said.

"I don't think I've changed," cut in Sims. "Sometimes it's a hassle. It reminds me of my recruiting days. I try to handle it all the same."

Sims was wearing an Orange Bowl jacket, an Oklahoma T-shirt and a Boston Red Sox baseball cap. "I think the "B" used to stand for Boston. Well, it stands for Billy now," Sims said.

The first person he planned to call Tuesday afternoon was his mother, who lives in St. Louis. "She probably already knows, but I want to call her. I'll take her to the banquet in New York. I think it's on Dec. 7," Sims said.

Oklahoma coach Barry Switzer was in Dallas "trying to get him (Sims) some help. I told him four years ago that if he came to Oklahoma he'd win the thing. It happens here, you know. No back in the country did what he did himself. He had no pre-season buildup or anything He did it all on his own," Switzer said. Switzer has indicated that the four OU co-captains will make the trip to New York for the banquet That means Roberts, Lott, Daryl Hunt and Phil Tabor will join Sims

"I'll rent me a tuxedo somewhere," Roberts said "I think I can get a tuxedo before we go," Sims added.

"I didn't come to Oklahoma because of what coach Switzer said about the Heisman," Sims said. "I didn't believe him. I came here because of the competition. There were a lot of places I could have gone and started right away. But I liked the competition."

Sims said he did have some thoughts of winning the Heisman last year. "In Texas, they have an award - I guess the little Heisman. They give it every year for the best high school player in Texas. My junior year in high school they gave it to Earl Campbell, then I won it the next year. Well, last year Earl Campbell won the Heisman. I figured it was my turn this year. I didn't tell anyone that, though," Sims said.

Lott, who was billed more as a Heisman candidate before the season than Sims, said he knew Sims would win "if they gave it to the guy who earned it on the field. I didn't have a lot of faith in it,

Continued on C-4

World Staff Photos by Johnny Walker and Jim Wolfe

En route to the Heisman Trophy, Billy Sims (inset) was a master of elusive running.

World Photo Layout by David Carman

TULSA WORLD

Sports

Wednesday,
Nov. 29, 1978

Holtz Insists He Will Stay at Arkansas

Unpredictable Lou Holtz, after weeks of silence, surprised football observers in Arkansas and Florida Tuesday by saying he intended to remain as coach of the Razorbacks.

"I have no plans to leave Arkansas today, tomorrow or next year," Holtz said on a radio show he tapes daily in Fayetteville. "There may be warmer climates, but there are no warmer people than the people in Arkansas."

Rumors that Holtz would resign and accept a similar position at Florida have been rampant for weeks. Holtz' refusal to defuse the rumors (As he

did when similar reports about Louisiana State surfaced) prompted many Arkansas insiders to conclude he would leave after the Razorbacks' Fiesta Bowl game against UCLA on Christmas Day.

Reportedly, Florida is preparing to fire coach Doug Dickey. It was reported Florida would also dump athletic director Ray Graves and offer Holtz both positions.

This plus the prospect of warm climate supposedly fascinated Holtz, who loathes cold weather and is not athletic director at Arkansas. Frank Broyles is.

But Holtz appeared to put to rest any supposition that he was not happy in his role under Broyles. He praised Broyles and others in Arkansas' athletic administration.

Oddly, Holtz' comments caused more surprise in Arkansas than Florida. A source in Florida familiar with the effort to hire Holtz said Florida was never confident of landing him The source also said Graves probably would not leave for at least another year.

Holtz said he was "tired" of the rumors. He said, "There is no way I can say I will spend the rest of my life in Arkansas." But

he assured he intended to return next season.

He explained further. "I think that is probably what people want to hear, but I can't say that, because of two reasons.

"No. 1, I feel the word is the most valuable thing a man has If I give you my word on something, and it does not come to pass, then there's no way in this world people can possibly respect somebody that says one thing and does something else.

"The second thing is, I have an obligation to my family. If I say I will never leave the University of Arkansas and an opportunity came along, maybe

another adventure or another fieldof endeavor, then I would have to do what I think is in the best interest of my family."

Holtz said he hoped his statement "will put an end to all the various and vicious rumors that people hear."

Holtz has also been rumored to be heir apparent to Woody Hayes at Ohio State. A native of Ohio, Holtz served on Hayes' staff in 1968 and considers Hayes a hero. But he has often said there was no basis for speculation he would be Hayes' successor.

Before coming to Arkansas, Holtz coached successfully in

underdog programs at William and Mary and North Carolina State. Then he spent one miserable year as coach of the professional New York Jets, before being hired to replace Broyles.

Holtz won several national coach-of-the-year awards in 1977, his first season at Arkansas. He took a lightly regarded team and directed it to an 11-1 record, concluding with a shocking 31-6 upset of Oklahoma in the Orange Bowl. Arkansas played the game without three backfield starters, suspended by Holtz for a dormitory incident, plus its best offensive lineman.

Billy Sims addresses the crowd during the unveiling of a statue of himself at Memorial Stadium in 2007.

"That was during a changing time in our country," Lott said. "We happened to be a part of that. I was able to be a part of that. Here I am, a black quarterback when there were maybe four in the country and not only was I embraced by the black community which backed me, but the thing that I am proud of also is the white people backed me too. They started to see that here is somebody that is black that we can relate to. Because of my background and the people I grew up around, I carried myself a certain way and they could also relate to me, so I was able to bring a group of people who had probably never been around black people to understand and want to follow this university because they are saying we have a little of both, black and white, and we are working together and everybody has a common goal of the university being the best it can be."

Defensive tackle Reggie Kinlaw was not one of the recruits Switzer "stole" from Texas. Kinlaw, who is from Miami, Fla., admired the Selmon brothers from afar.

"I said, 'I'm going to be like those guys,' " Kinlaw said. "And Barry helped get me there."

Kinlaw said Switzer had a knack for saying things that would happen – eventually, if not immediately.

"As he stood up on top of the tower and watched practice, he called me a jackass freshman," Kinlaw said. "He said, 'Jackass freshman Reggie Kinlaw, if you practice like that every day, you will be a two-time All-American.' And it came true."

Kinlaw said players liked to "blast" Bar-Kays and O'Jays music before games. An assistant coach once walked over and ordered the volume to be turned down. "Barry politely walked over there and turned it back up and said, 'Hey, let them enjoy the music.' He is a players' coach."

That's plural, as in players.

"We had a lot of talent, man," Kinlaw said. "I just was blessed to get there at the right time. The year I came in we had Billy and Thomas and Kenny King and Greg Roberts and Daryl Hunt and George Cumby – all these guys from Texas."

Billy Sims carries the ball against West Virginia on Sept. 16, 1978.

Lott said the talent level was incredible.

"I was eight deep on the depth chart when I got there and there were two guys behind me. There was no scholarship (limit prior to 1973). When you are talking about eight deep, we are talking about quarterback, fullback, both halfbacks. And everybody was All-State, All-City, All-American, All-Conererence. They were all something from wherever they came from."

Switzer promised Sims he would earn a degree and win a Heisman Trophy (both of which he did) if he came to Oklahoma.

"Of course he told Kenny King and Thomas Lott and all these other people the same damn story," Sims said, laughing.

Sims, who won the Heisman Trophy in 1978 and was runner-up in 1979, said he thinks anybody in OU's backfield during that era could have won a Heisman because the Sooners were just that good.

"Probably the best thing to ever happen for me was to come to Oklahoma," he said. "What I know now, because I didn't know it back then, is you surround yourself with other great players, just like in business, and you give yourself a chance to be successful."

Sims said there were so many great players that you hoped someone would get hurt in practice just so you would get an opportunity.

"That's how stacked we were," he said. "You had guys there that could have been starting at other universities. They all wanted to come to Oklahoma because of one guy."

Said Webb: "That's what a lot of people – even the administration – didn't realize is people came there to play for Barry. They didn't come there to play for the University of Oklahoma. The Internet isn't like it is now. The (OU) brand wasn't necessarily known that well outside. We had heard of Bud Wilkinson, but we were all young country boys. You got there and you played for Barry. That's what we knew. You would have run through a wall for the man."

About that Pearl beer story: Blevins said OU assistant coach Gary Gibbs had made a home visit before Switzer. Gibbs was offered a Pearl beer. It's possible that Switzer rummaged through a trash can or saw a trash can overflowing with Pearl beer cans. But Blevins suspects Gibbs tipped off Switzer that he would be offered "nasty" beer during the home visit.

"My dad was a big Pearl beer drinker," Blevins said. "I don't know if he bought it because he liked it or he knew that me and my sister wouldn't drink it."

Switzer, who has gotten ample mileage out of the story over the years, ran into Blevins in New Orleans decades after his playing career was over and greeted Blevins by saying "they don't have any Pearl beer here."

Switzer didn't miss many tricks.

Said Blevins about his recruitment: "Just the little things he would do ... I'm sure he did a lot of mothers this way, but he called my mom on her birthday."

CHAPTER 7

Recession

"Football coaching is like a terminal disease. It is going to get you sooner or later. You just don't know when."

— *Barry Switzer*

OU head coach Barry Switzer takes it hard on the sidelines in Dallas as his team found the going rough against the University of Texas on Oct. 10, 1981. The Longhorns defeated the Sooners, 34-14. Oklahoma lost four games in each season from 1981 through 1983. To fans, the sky was falling.

PUSHING PAST STRUGGLES

On Oct. 27, 1984, Oklahoma was without injured starting quarterback Danny Bradley.

Bradley's replacement, 17-year-old freshman Troy Aikman, made his college debut and completed 2-of-14 passes for eight yards in a 28-11 loss to unranked Kansas. Probably, some folks immediately jumped to the conclusion that the Aikman kid would never amount to anything.

Being upset by a 22-point underdog was the second-worst thing to happen to the Sooners that weekend.

Hours after the game, senior safety Keith Stanberry was cruising across railroad tracks in Norman when the Datsun he was driving careened out of control. The car didn't stop until it was guillotined by a telephone pole. Freshman cornerback Andre Johnson was in the vehicle when it got mangled. Their injuries were catastrophic. Anyone who saw the wreckage, or photos of it, knew it could have been worse.

"We nearly had two dead players this morning," Barry Switzer told the Oklahoman's Bob Hersom. "They shouldn't have survived that."

Let's put things in perspective and clarify that there are different kinds of survival. Switzer said those words not long after his own survival had been in question.

Switzer won at a ridiculous rate during his first eight seasons as head coach. From 1973 through 1980, the Sooners were 83-9-2 with two national championships and they were oh-so-close to others.

What kind of job security did that buy him?

Troy Aikman, a 17-year-old OU freshman, replaced injured starting quarterback Danny Bradley in 1984. In his college debut, he completed 2-of-14 passes for eight yards in a loss to unranked Kansas. He is shown during Oklahoma's 1985 game against Miami in which he was sidelined by a broken ankle.

OU's Keith Stanberry (19) appears to intercept a pass intended for Texas' Bill Bryant (80) in the final moments of a 1984 game. Officials ruled that Stanberry bobbled the ball until he was out of bounds. The game ended in a 15-15 tie. Stanberry was seriously injured in a car accident two weeks later.

"Like Barry says, feeding the monster is tough," former assistant coach Merv Johnson said. "One or two losses, you are treading on thin ice."

Four losses? You better know who your friends are on the board of regents.

OU went 7-4-1 in 1981, 8-4 in 1982 and 8-4 in 1983. The sky was falling.

"Most people think that OU just went 7-4-1," Switzer said at a booster function. "But there has been a delayed reaction. The president of the university has resigned since then, Penn Square Bank has folded and the oil business is going downhill. I know it was the 7-4-1 that did it."

Things that might not be a big deal when you are winning at a crazy rate all of a sudden get scrutinized when you coach teams that are merely mortal.

For instance: It made news in May 1982 when Switzer used OU stationery and a university postage meter to send letters promoting a country singer he had decided to represent. Switzer said at the time that he hoped to do for John Kelly what former Texas coach Darrell Royal had done for Willie Nelson.

Was it kosher to use university postal assets for non-university business? Switzer defended himself, saying in an Associated Press story he had designed the stationery years earlier and paid for his own postage.

"I do have such visibility that there are people who question everything I do," he said. "Here I am trying to help a kid that's a pretty good talent."

Switzer's mistake might have been sending a promotional letter about Kelly to a radio station in Austin, Texas, home of the Longhorns. It was the Austin station that challenged the use of the stationery and postage.

Fair or unfair, it was speculated that OU was losing more games than normal be-

"The president of the university has resigned since then, Penn Square Bank has folded and the oil business is going downhill. I know it was the 7-4-1 that did it."

— *Barry Switzer*

cause Switzer had too many things going on outside of football.

"You bet I worked at some of my interest investments," Switzer told The Tulsa Tribune in 1982. "You know why? The way I look at it (is) you are going to get fired. Football coaching is like a terminal disease. It is going to get you sooner or later. You just don't know when."

People close to Switzer will tell you that, even in retirement, he has a million irons in the fire.

"I think Barry has always been the kind of guy who can't sit still," Lacewell said. "He can fish. ... But if the fish aren't biting in five minutes, he ain't staying. And golf, my God, it will drive him crazy. So he has got to be doing something all the time. He's always selling something. Barry has always pictured himself a businessman."

Fans often have a hard time grasping that winning isn't a birthright and that other teams have good players, too. Nonconference losses during the recession years came to USC (twice), West Virginia (quarterbacked by future pro Jeff Hostetler) and Ohio State.

"We probably didn't recruit as well (at that time) and we were piddling with leaving some of the wishbone stuff, which obviously we knew a lot more about than we did other offenses," former assistant Merv Johnson said. "And I think our talent level dropped off a little bit in '82 maybe and '83 certainly."

OU temporarily discarded the wishbone to tailor an offense for Marcus Dupree. An All-everything running back recruit

> "I think Barry has always been the kind of guy who can't sit still. He can fish. ... But if the fish aren't biting in five minutes, he ain't staying. And golf, my God, it will drive him crazy."
>
> — *Larry Lacewell, former OU assistant head coach*

Opposite: Marcus Dupree celebrates after scoring in the OU-Texas game on Oct. 9, 1982. OU won, 28-22. Dupree was dubbed "The Best That Never Was" in a 2010 ESPN documentary.

from Philadelphia, Miss., Dupree was dubbed "The Best That Never Was" in a 2010 ESPN documentary.

Dupree was a man-child with freakish talent. But Switzer had issues with Dupree's work ethic and they became embattled. Dupree lasted one "wow" season and part of another before going back to his home state. In between, Sports Illustrated made Dupree a cover subject over the objections of Switzer.

Years later, and with benefit of hindsight, Switzer and Dupree wouldn't mind a do-over. But the hatchet is long buried. Dupree said he was the general manager of an arena football team in Shreveport, La., when he called Switzer and asked the coach if he would show up for a pre-game coin toss ceremony. Switzer agreed, then got emotional after the game while talking about how his relationship with Dupree had gone awry.

> "People go through things and time brings about change and my mom has always said time brings about healing."
>
> — *Marcus Dupree*

"People go through things and time brings about change and my mom has always said time brings about healing," Dupree said.

Amid the OU recession, rumors circulated that Switzer would be replaced by Dick Vermeil. It wasn't the first time Switzer had dealt with exit rumors. Lacewell and Switzer feuded after the 1977 season and Lacewell resigned. Assistant coaches Gene Hochevar and Jerry Pettibone also resigned. At a subsequent varsity-alumni game in the spring of 1978, sports writers showed up in anticipation that the head coach was on the verge of resigning. False alarm.

After the 1983 season, Switzer sought out regents to squash a movement to push him out the door and got what sounded like a stay of execution. His contract usually got rolled over for a continuous five-year deal. In February 1984, regents approved

Marcus Dupree (left) is shown in Norman with Barry Switzer in August 1983.
Dupree was a man-child from Philadelphia, Miss., with freakish talent.

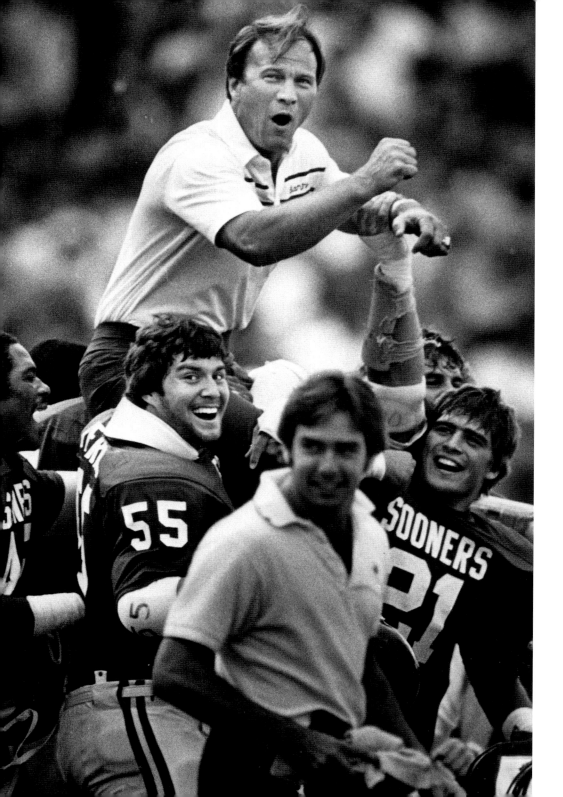

"only" a four-year deal.

When reporters visited Norman for the Big Eight Skywriters Tour in 1984, Switzer said, "What are you guys trying to find out – how many games I've got to win to keep my job? I don't know. You're asking the wrong guy."

OU won nine games in 1984 and was in the national championship conversation before an Orange Bowl loss to Washington. Pursuing a crown was the last thing on Switzer's mind when he hustled to the hospital to visit Stanberry and Andre Johnson after their car accident. Their injuries were so severe that their dreams of playing in the NFL crashed that same night.

Johnson, who had just started his college career, should have been a candidate to feel sorry

The Sooners lift Barry Switzer as they celebrate their 28-22 victory over the Texas Longhorns on Oct. 9, 1982.

for himself and return home to Houston. Switzer didn't let that happen.

Johnson told this story: When something tragic happens in anyone's life, others may sometimes neglect to make contact in order to avoid uncomfortable conversations.

Switzer did the opposite, asking folks, "Has anybody seen Andre?" And, because things start at the top, that rubbed off on others.

"If you wouldn't have known I was injured, you would have thought I was a guy that was starting every weekend because that's the way I was treated," Johnson said.

"Barry Switzer kept me a part of the team. I traveled. I went to Orange Bowls. I did everything that everybody else did. I came and went as I pleased throughout the facilities. I was just one of the guys."

Johnson said he was never taken off athletic scholarship and that Switzer encouraged him to get a degree and work hard in the weight room just in case a return to the playing field was possible.

At the time, Johnson was convinced he would play again. As an adult, he can be honest with himself that his injuries were too much to overcome.

Taking advantage of access to tutors available to other student-athletes, Johnson graduated with a political science degree in December 1988.

"Barry Switzer kept me a part of the team. I traveled. I went to Orange Bowls. I did everything that everybody else did. I came and went as I pleased throughout the facilities. I was just one of the guys."

— *former OU player Andre Johnson*

"You see guys like Andre Johnson and Keith Stanberry, who got devastated in a car wreck that just completely destructed their careers and their ability to perform athletically," former teammate Jon Phillips said. "Coach Switzer really stuck with those guys and personally made sure that they stuck with it and stuck with their grades and stuck with their classes and got their degrees and if you run into either one of them today, you would be like, 'Wow.' They are successful."

Johnson is in pharmaceutical sales in Texas and, because he shares a name with the Houston Texans' star receiver, he has to explain he's not "that guy." But it gives him an excuse to say he played football at OU and he gets questions about what it was like to play for Switzer.

"Being in Texas, they are looking for me to say something bad," he said. "And I really disappoint them when I tell them my version of what I call the truth, which is really the truth. He's a good guy."

Oklahoma head coach Barry Switzer gives last-minute instructions to his team in Miami on Dec. 31, 1980. Oklahoma defeated Florida State University, 18-17, in the Orange Bowl on New Year's Day.

CHAPTER 8

The Comeback

"If I had said in my first year that I was going after Bud's record, you would have put me over at (a mental hospital). You don't start out with those types of goals."

— *Barry Switzer on surpassing Bud Wilkinson as OU's winningest coach*

Oklahoma coach Barry Switzer gets a ride from jubilant players Tony Casillas (left) and Jeff Tupper in Miami on Jan. 2, 1986. Oklahoma was ranked No. 3 going into the Orange Bowl, but their 25-10 victory over No. 1 Penn State, coupled with Miami's loss in the Sugar Bowl, vaulted the Sooners to their sixth national championship.

A SECOND WAVE OF SUCCESS

Jon Phillips laughed. His father wasn't laughing.

The occasion? Barry Switzer made a recruiting visit to Jenks, Okla., while restocking the Sooners' roster in the 1980s.

"It was probably 60 degrees outside and he shows up in this thing," Phillips said.

The "thing" was a fur coat.

"He had been to our high school that day because that was one of the things he would do," Phillips said.

"He would show up at your high school and he would walk in right at the most crowded time and saunter through the halls in this big, long fur coat and he would have an entourage of a couple of other coaches with him and they would make their way to the counselor's office and the principal's office and then the coach's office so that everybody at school would know that Barry Switzer was there."

Switzer was still wearing fur when he showed up at Phillips' home. The coach, in full swagger mode, made a sales pitch and left. Immediately after the door shut behind Switzer, a furious dad called the coach every name under the sun.

"Barry's presence and persona and personality and my dad's personality were oil and water," Phillips said. "My dad couldn't get past that at first."

No way, declared dad, was his son going to Oklahoma.

The rest of the story? Two sons – Jon and younger brother Anthony – went to OU and started on the offensive line.

> "Wilkinson was country club. Switzer is main street."
>
> — *Tulsa World sports editor Bill Connors*

Oklahoma State University head coach Pat Jones (left) congratulates OU's Barry Switzer following the Sooners' 29-10 victory in 1987. The win put Switzer in the record book as Oklahoma's winningest coach at that time. Bob Stoops surpassed Switzer in 2013.

"He would show up at your high school and ... saunter through the halls in this big, long fur coat ... and they (Switzer and staff) would make their way to the counselor's office and the principal's office and then the coach's office so that everybody at school would know that Barry Switzer was there."

— *Jon Phillips, former OU player*

The Phillips brothers, though they attended high school in Oklahoma, did not grow up hoping to play for OU. They spent childhood years in Tennessee and were fans of the Volunteers. Vols coach Johnny Majors did not wear a fur coat when he made a home visit.

Jon took a recruiting trip to Norman. Dad picked up Jon afterward and a car ride was quiet until they got close to home.

Dad: "You're going to go there, aren't you?"

Jon: "Yeah, I am."

The car ride got noisy.

Jon put his name on the dotted line as a member of the signing day class of 1983. The best thing players in that recruiting class did was, counterintuitively, to avoid making an immediate impact.

Former assistant coach Merv Johnson said Switzer, never mind that he was in the midst of three consecutive four-loss seasons, "was smart enough and strong enough ... to take a very good recruiting class in '83 and redshirt them. He had all those linebackers and a bunch of people back as redshirt freshmen in '84."

OU redshirted 21 freshmen in 1983. Three of the redshirts became All-Americans and seven (Brian Bosworth, Greg Johnson, Troy Johnson,

Spencer Tillman soars over the goal line for Oklahoma's first touchdown in their game against Southern Methodist University on Dec. 7, 1985. Tillman, an All-America running back, was captain of the 1985 team and later played professional football with the Houston Oilers and San Francisco 49ers.

Brian Bosworth makes a tackle in the OU-Missouri game on Nov. 8, 1986, in Norman. "Last one?" is written on his cleat, referring to concerns about a looming suspension. The NCAA barred Bosworth and two teammates from participating in the Orange Bowl that year after the players tested positive for steroid use. He played two seasons in the NFL before retiring due to injuries.

Dante Jones, Darrell Reed, Jon Phillips and Caesar Rentie) were drafted.

The Sooners flirted with a national championship when those redshirts debuted in 1984. That was the first step toward Switzer's second golden era. In 1985, 1986 and 1987, his teams lost a total of three games – all to the Miami Hurricanes.

Switzer plucked prospects from his home state in restoring the roar, sending assistant coach Charley North to Arkansas to snare Parade All-American tight end Keith Jackson, offensive lineman Mark Hutson and defensive lineman Curtice Williams in 1984.

Williams said Switzer (of course) wore a fur coat when he made a recruiting visit to Pine Bluff, Ark. Switzer stressed to Williams that the Sooners were all about championships.

Williams redshirted in 1984 and was part of a national championship team in 1985. His welcome-to-college-football moment came when starter Tony Casillas suffered a knee injury against Texas in the third game of the '85 season and Williams was sent in to replace him. Butterflies were knocked out of Williams the first time he got hit.

"I had played a little bit in the first two games, but mop-up duty is nothing like going against Texas, going into a rivalry game like that," he said. "And then, coming off that, the next week I've got to go out and line up against Miami. You talk about getting thrown into the fire."

Freshman quarterback Jamelle Holieway was thrown into the fire, too. Starting quarterback Troy Aikman, whose strength

"It was just a great time to be at OU. From 1985 to 1988 were the years that I played. We were 42-6 and won three Big Eight championships and a national championship and probably should have won more than one. But we had a great run and we had a great time doing it."

— *Former player Anthony Phillips*

was an NFL arm, sustained a season-ending injury when one of his ankles was broken by Miami's Jerome Brown. OU lost the game, but found its next great wishbone quarterback when Holieway came off the bench. The Sooners swept the remainder of their games and beat Penn State in the Orange Bowl.

Another discovery during the championship season was "the Boz."

Brian Bosworth played well enough in 1984 to be chosen the Big Eight's defensive newcomer of the year. On page 30 of the 1985 OU football media guide, there's a mug shot of Bosworth with a normal (at least for the 1980s) mane. He wasn't Boz yet.

"He was just Brian," Williams said.

The movie "Commando" was released early in the 1985 season. Players ventured to the theater to see Arnold Schwarzenegger kick butt. Schwarzenegger's character had hair spiked on the top and trimmed on the sides.

"The next weekend, Brian had his hair cut like that and Paul Migliazzo started calling him the Boz," Williams said. "And that's how the Boz got started."

Bosworth's penchant for drawing attention to himself was among the factors that landed him in Switzer's doghouse. But, as is often the case with Switzer, grudges are temp jobs.

"Coach is one of those guys who is always going to find something good in you," former player Louis Oubre said.

OU lost a nationally televised regular season showdown at Miami in 1986 and "settled" for an 11-1 season. Beating Arkan-

> "The next weekend, Brian had his hair cut like that and Paul Migliazzo started calling him the Boz. And that's how the Boz got started."
>
> *— Defensive lineman Curtice Williams, on how Brian Bosworth became "the Boz" after watching an Arnold Schwarzenegger film*

All-America linebacker and Butkus Award winner Brian Bosworth became known as "the Boz" after getting a haircut similar to Arnold Schwarzenegger's in the 1985 action movie "Commando."

Nose guard Curtice Williams was called on to substitute for injured star Tony Casillas in the third game of the 1985 championship season against Texas. Williams said that he had played some in his first two years at Oklahoma, but it was nothing like "going into a rivalry game like that."

sas 42-8 in the Orange Bowl permitted Switzer to get even for an embarrassing Orange Bowl loss to his alma mater nine years earlier.

Anthony Phillips said you never knew which direction Switzer's pregame talks might go. This one was different.

"He basically stood up and said, 'Hey guys, I don't ever ask you to do anything for me. But I have been living with this '78 OU-Arkansas Orange Bowl game for way too long. I want you guys to go out there and kick their ass.' It was one of those (speeches). And it was good. That was a great memory."

Oklahoma went unbeaten during the 1987 regular season and was outscoring opponents by 45.5 points per game before Holieway sustained a knee injury in a Nov. 7 game against Oklahoma State. Minus Holieway, the Sooners didn't score more than 17 points in any of three remaining games, including a 20-14 Orange Bowl loss to Miami with a national championship at stake.

Going 33-3 in a three-season flurry helped Switzer achieve the unthinkable. He caught Bud.

A college football icon, Bud Wilkinson went 145-29-4 at Oklahoma. Switzer surpassed Wilkinson as OU's winningest coach during the 1987 season.

"If I had said in my first year that I was going after Bud's record, you would have put me over at (a mental hospital)," Switzer said. "You don't start out with those types of goals."

Bill Connors, who served as the Tulsa World's sports editor from 1959-1994, treated readers to these observations in 1987:

- "Wilkinson was country club. Switzer is main street. Wilkinson was button-down royalty who would never be caught in public without a coat and tie. Switzer is a neighbor who goes to press conferences without a tie and sometimes without socks. The supermarket cashier from Cherokee who would not have the nerve to introduce himself to Wilkinson is not reluctant to ask Switzer to stop on his way to the team bus and have his picture made with the man's family."

> "I just always appreciated his honesty. He would always tell you straight up. ... You always knew where you stood with him and it wasn't always pleasant. And he liked to have fun. He liked people that had fun."
>
> — *Former player Jon Phillips on Switzer*

- "There are still some who think of Switzer as Roger Maris. Wilkinson will always be Babe Ruth. There is a mystique about the urbane, handsome Wilkinson that Switzer cannot match. And Wilkinson was more of a hero in his profession. He was an establishment figure, accepted by the lions and in demand to give clinics and write books."

- "Switzer was an Xs and Os superstar as an assistant and his ability to evaluate teach and motivate is extraordinary. But

Freshman Jamelle Holieway became OU's starting quarterback after Troy Aikman's ankle was broken in the 1985 game against Miami. He led OU to eight straight wins that season, including an Orange Bowl victory over Penn State.

he lost favor with the establishment as a rookie coach (brashness on his part or jealousy on their part?) and his public passion about the importance of recruiting has created a mythical image that he is a pushbutton coach who wins only on talent. Hence, he does not have the stature Wilkinson enjoyed."

• "Just as Wilkinson was ideal for the 50s when obedient players were raised on Ozzie and Harriet and Jack Benny, Switzer is ideal for players who grew up in permissive times on Miami Vice and Richard Pryor."

Jon Phillips' father, Jerry, eventually warmed up to the fur-bearing coach from the Richard Pryor era. Said Jon, "He realized there was a different side than the showy, outgoing recruiter that came into our house."

Jon Phillips said he found Switzer to be charming and honest. Even when Switzer said something that sounded like exaggeration, it still seemed within the realm of possibility. For instance: Hey, Holieway. If you come to OU, the wishbone may

OU tight end Keith Jackson (88) scores a touchdown against Oklahoma State in 1984. Jackson, a Little Rock, Ark., native, was named to the 1983 Parade All-American Team and went on to play for the Philadelphia Eagles, Miami Dolphins and Green Bay Packers.

come back and you'll win a national championship.

Added Jon Phillips, "I just always appreciated his honesty. He would always tell you straight up. ... You always knew where you stood with him and it wasn't always pleasant. And he liked to have fun. He liked people that had fun."

University of Miami coach Jimmy Johnson (left) and Oklahoma coach Barry Switzer are shown during a news conference in December 1987 before their two teams met in the Orange Bowl to determine the national championship. Miami won, 20-14.

Maybe too much fun was had when Phillips' little brother Anthony and his Jenks teammate Richard Davis came to Norman for a recruiting visit when they were high school seniors. A party broke out and significant property damage included a sink being pulled out of a bathroom wall.

TULSA DAILY WORLD

71st Year—No. 109   *Final Home Edition*   TULSA, OKLAHOMA, SATURDAY, JANUARY 3, 1976   *Single Copy—15c*   40 PAGES —3 PARTS

Sooners Are No. 1!
2 Major Polls Cast
Votes for Big Red

World Wire Reports

The University of Oklahoma Sooners survived a mid-season upset defeat and exploited Ohio State's loss in the Rose Bowl to garner the national championship titles in two major wire services' post season football polls Friday.

The Sooners were voted No. 1 by the Associated Press, the United Press International's coaches poll and also were named winner of the Grantland Rice Trophy by the Football Writers Association of America.

THE SOONERS, WHO DEFEATED Michigan 14-6 in the Orange Bowl Thursday after then top-ranked Ohio State had lost 23-10 to UCLA in the Rose Bowl, received 54½ first-place votes in the AP poll and 1,257 total points Friday from a nationwide panel of 63 sports writers and sportscasters. OU was voted No. 1 by the AP last year.

The Sooners, 11-1, were well ahead of No. 2 ranked Arizona State, 12-0. The Sun Devils, one of only two undefeated and untied teams in major college football this season, collected five first-place AP votes and 1,038 points for their highest finish ever.

Alabama lost its opening game of the season to Missouri then won its next 11 games, including Wednesday night's 13-6 victory over Penn State in the Sugar Bowl, and that earned the Crimson Tide the No. 3 spot in the AP poll. They had 3½ first place votes and 954 points.

THAT WAS SEVEN POINTS MORE than fourth-ranked Ohio State, which had held the No. 1 rating from the fifth week of the 1975 season until Friday. The Buckeyes lost the spot because of

THE DUAL NATIONAL TITLE WAS Oklahoma's first since the Bud Wilkinson era of the mid-1950s, but it was the Sooners' fourth title overall and tied them with Southern California for most championships in the 26-year history of the UPI ratings. Oklahoma previously won UPI national titles in 1950, 1955 and 1956.

The UPI's top 10-list changed dramatically following the post-season bowls in which half of the previous top 10 teams were beaten.

In addition to Arizona State, which moved up four places in the final ratings, UCLA and Arkansas made the most notable gains. UCLA used its stunning victory over Ohio State to climb eight spots to No. 5 while Ar-

See Sooners Finish on A-4

Woman Has Healthy Baby
After Plunge Into River

CHARLESTON, W.Va. — A 20-year-old woman gave birth to a healthy baby Friday, 2½ hours after her car plunged into the icy Elk River.

"God must have timed that just right. It was a miracle," Dr. Curtis White said after delivering the six-pound, two-ounce boy to Janet Keaton at Charleston Memorial Hospital.

Her husband, George, 23, of Clendenin was driving her to the hospital when he tried to pass a bus on U.S. 119 near Elkview, hit a slick spot in the road and plunged into the river, officials said.

Keaton said neither his wife nor a friend with them, Olen Myers, 19, could swim and he pushed both through the broken rear window of his station wagon.

"When I surfaced," Keaton said, "all I could hear was my wife screaming for help. If I had not seen this happen, I wouldn't have believed anyone could have lived through it."

Mrs Keaton was unhurt. Keaton was treated for minor face and head injuries and Myers suffered a broken arm, hospital officials said.

Heavy Snows Hit

Switzer strikes a No. 1 pose Thursday night. Friday the polls agreed.   —Associated Press WIREPHOTO

8 Per Cent Level Placed
On Tax Assessments

By DAVID AVERILL   TULSA SCHOOL OFFICIALS HAVE   ONE COUNTY IS AT THAT LEVEL,

The Tulsa World front page of Jan. 3, 1976, is topped by a story about the Sooners being voted national champions, with a photo of Barry Switzer giving the No. 1 sign. Ten years later, Oklahoma won its third national championship under Switzer, with an 11-1 record and an Orange Bowl victory over Penn State.

The recruiting hosts, Jon Phillips and Al Laurita, dreaded an inevitable meeting with Switzer the following Monday. Phillips got as far as the weight room before strength coach Pete Martinelli said, "Um, you need to see coach Switzer."

Laurita was sitting in Switzer's office when Jon arrived. Switzer, agitated, showed them a bill for damages. But the Sooners signed both recruits and Anthony Phillips became a consensus All-American in 1988. Call it a good investment.

"It was just a great time to be at OU," Anthony Phillips said. "From 1985 to 1988 were the years that I played. We were 42-6 and won three Big Eight championships and a national championship and probably should have won more than one. But we had a great run and we had a great time doing it."

Barry Switzer is shown during the OU-Nebraska game in 1987. From 1985-87, his teams amassed a 33-3 record and helped him surpass Bud Wilkinson as OU's winningest coach.

CHAPTER 9

Resignation

"David Swank never fired me and never asked me for my resignation. ... All he ever presented to me were accusations and fabrications that were false."

— Barry Switzer, 20 years after resigning

A sign at Big Red Sales, reading "Thanks Barry Oklahoma is still Switzerland," reflected the sentiment of many OU fans upon hearing of Switzer's resignation.

END OF A REIGN

Barry Switzer turned 50 on Oct. 5, 1987. He dropped half a hundred on Father Time. And, as far as he was concerned, he was nowhere near finished coaching at the University of Oklahoma.

"There is nothing else I want to do," he told the Tulsa World. "I enjoy it. The little boy in me allows me to relate to the players. I think I can coach 10 more years. I just want to keep winning and 10 years from now have six national championships."

The same article said Switzer's multiple television and radio shows permitted him to boost his annual income to what Madonna makes in a week. Two years removed from a national championship and a few months shy of playing for another, he had fed the monster enough victories to feel secure on the crimson throne.

Then came the 1988 season. And Switzer was gone.

Coaching is the ultimate what-have-you-done-for-me-lately profession, but Switzer's exit had nothing to do with numbers on a scoreboard. The Sooners were 9-1 in his farewell season before dropping a regular season finale to Nebraska and a Citrus Bowl to Clemson.

Then came a wave of bad news.

OU was placed on NCAA probation in December 1988.

Cornerback Jerry Parks was arrested for shooting (and wounding) teammate Zarak Peters on Jan. 13, 1989. The shooting occurred in an athletic dormitory.

Eight days later, an alleged sexual assault in the dorm led to three players (Nigel Clay, Bernard Hall and Glen Bell) going to

"There is nothing else I want to do. I enjoy it. The little boy in me allows me to relate to the players. I think I can coach 10 more years. I just want to keep winning and 10 years from now have six national championships."

—*Barry Switzer in 1987*

Quarterback Charles Thompson (6) is shown during OU's September 26, 1987, game with TU. Thompson was arrested for selling 17 grams of cocaine to an undercover FBI agent. He pleaded guilty and served 17 months at a federal prison in Big Spring, Texas.

trial. Clay and Hall were convicted. Bell was acquitted.

And exactly one month after the shooting, quarterback Charles Thompson was arrested for selling cocaine to an undercover agent. Thompson appeared on a Sports Illustrated cover in handcuffs and wearing orange prison coveralls. "Oklahoma: A Sordid Story" was the headline atop the cover.

Switzer found himself in the crosshairs. Editorials in Oklahoma newspapers called for him to resign. He reasoned that it shouldn't have been necessary to make team rules about things that are against the law.

Meanwhile, allies made it clear they had Switzer's back. Contacted by the Los Angeles Times, Switzer's secretary, Kay Day, said there were about 1,000 letters of support piled in stacks near her desk. The Times' story said a NASA scientist, a nun and baseball star Reggie Jackson were among people calling to wish Switzer well.

Would Switzer survive? That was the question, and it was asked a lot. Former player Anthony Phillips, whose final semester coincided with the perfect storm of 1989, said you couldn't walk around the stadium at that time because you would be mobbed by reporters.

The biggest show of support – and it was for intended for public consumption – came at the Oklahoma City Marriott on Feb. 22, 1989. It happened two days after members of the 1949 OU football team announced they were scrapping a 40th anniversary reunion.

"Because of the latest inexcusable, disgusting and embarrassing events that have occurred in the football program, I do not plan to be a part of a reunion on campus until a drastic change in leadership takes place," Jim Owens, a co-captain of the 1949 team, wrote in a letter to university brass.

In response, players coached by Switzer hastily worked the phones in a pre-cellphone era and urged everyone to assemble at the Marriott to back the embattled coach and athletic director Donnie Duncan. This was the Switzer version of everyone showing up at George Bailey's home at the end of "It's A Wonderful Life."

> "Because of the latest inexcusable, disgusting and embarrassing events that have occurred in the football program, I do not plan to be a part of a reunion on campus until a drastic change in leadership takes place."
>
> — *Jim Owens, a co-captain of the 1949 team*

Heisman winners Steve Owens and Billy Sims co-chaired the committee of supporters and they were joined on a dais at the Mariott by J.C. Watts and Spencer Tillman. Owens read a statement which had been signed by more than 70 former players, many of whom were in attendance. Among them was Phillips, who told the Tulsa World that anti-Switzer sentiment reminded him of how justice must have been doled out in the Old West.

"No jury, no trial, just go hang somebody," he said. "Everybody is out to see blood."

TULSA WORLD

84th Year—No. 277 Final Home Edition Tulsa, Oklahoma, Tuesday, June 20, 1989 ENTIRE CONTENTS © 1989 WORLD PUBLISHING CO. 35 Cents

Switzer Ends Reign as OU Coach

By Clay Henry
World Staff Writer

NORMAN — Barry Switzer became accustomed to stepping off an airplane at Miami, Fla., for the Orange Bowl football game with dozens of members of the national media ready to roast him.

"OK," he would say. "You guys want me to wear the black hat, OK."

Monday afternoon, Switzer hung up his black hat.

Switzer, the winningest active head coach in Division I collegiate football, stepped down at the University of Oklahoma when a stormy six months of NCAA sanctions and felony charges against Sooner players left him "drained" and "without the enthusiasm to go compete in the arena."

Switzer's resignation was effective immediately: The Sooners were moving quickly to name a replacement. Athletic Director Donnie Duncan made a recommendation to the Athletic Council on Monday afternoon. Interim President David Swank said he would take that name before the Board of Regents early Tuesday. An announcement on the new coach was expected at a 9 a.m. Tuesday news conference. It is believed Duncan's choice was defensive coordinator Gary Gibbs.

Switzer promised he would "never coach at the college level again." He said anything he would do at another school would "deplete or detract from" his 16-year record of 157-29-43. The Sooners won 12 Big Eight Conference crowns and were national champs in 1974, 1975 and 1985 under Switzer.

FAST TAKE

University of Oklahoma football coach Barry Switzer quit Monday. He said problems in the OU football program left him drained, and without enthusiasm to compete. More Fast Takes on A-4.

■ Life without Barry Switzer at the helm of the OU Sooners seems a little bit emptier, lifelong fans said Monday. "I can't hardly believe it," said Tulsan Scott Smith. "It's kind of like it took something out of me. Barry Switzer is Oklahoma football." B-1

■ Shock waves rumbled through college football Monday when Barry Switzer stepped down. B-2

---

watered at the end of his seven-minute prepared statement), Switzer entered the room cracking jokes. He found time for some one-liners during a question-and-answer session before a throng of former players, OU assistant coaches and supporters which joined the media at the Jack Santee Lounge in Memorial Stadium.

When pressed for his future plans, Switzer laughed, "I may write a book," an obvious reference to the recent announcement by former OU player Brian Bosworth that a second expose on the Sooner program was in the works.

Athletic Director Donnie Duncan welcomed Switzer's help with the OU program.

"I'm not sure what his capacity will

---

said he had known for "at least two weeks" that a decision was imminent, but was not 100 percent until "about 1:30 Friday morning."

Switzer telephoned Duncan early Thursday afternoon to ask for a meeting, but both had commitments which prevented a hookup.

"He had tried to get me and then I tried to get back to him that night, but it wasn't until 1:30 when I got him," Duncan said. "I picked him up in my car."

Switzer, Duncan and OU interim President David Swank were all adamant that there had been no pressure for the coach to resign from anyone at OU. And speculation that Richard Van Horn, to be sworn in as president next month, played a part in Switzer's decision was met with rejection, too.

"I've met Dr. Van Horn one time, at an alumni meeting in Houston," Switzer said. "It was a very positive meeting.

"The only one involved was Barry Switzer."

Duncan was not surprised at Switzer's decision. The AD said he saw it coming even before the NCAA sanctions at season's end and the off-field problems with the OU players.

"He came to me after the loss at Southern Cal," Duncan said. "He talked to me then about retiring. He's been up and down since then. I think it all reached a certain level this week where he wanted to do something."

In his prepared statement, Switzer said he "deeply regrets the series of events which have focused so much adverse publicity" on the football program. Several players were charged early this year with crimes involving drugs, guns and sexual assault.

He thanked the many OU fans and personal supporters for the encouragement during this time.

"You gave me the belief that I had the energy level to carry the program

The resignation of OU head football coach Barry Switzer was front-page news across Oklahoma, including the June 20, 1989, edition of the Tulsa World. Switzer's exit had nothing to do with his team's performance on the football field. Editorials in Oklahoma newspapers had called for the coach to step down after NCAA probation and criminal charges against several players. By contrast, a poll in the rival state of Nebraska showed that only 28 percent of registered voters there thought Switzer should resign.

Twenty-five years later, Phillips said that was a good representation of how he felt.

"Like I have always said over the years, any time you get 100 kids together – 100 young men from various parts of the country and different demographics – unfortunately you are always going to get a few bad apples," he said. "You are going to get some that go the wrong way. I think you could take a slice of 100 young men at that age anywhere in the country and you are probably going to have about the same percentage of ones that go the wrong way or make a mistake."

Former player Jon Phillips, Anthony's brother, was part of the Marriott crew. Switzer wasn't there, but sent letters to those who were. Wrote Switzer: "Dear Jon: Your love and pride for the Sooner program has been demonstrated many times in past years to me. I witnessed a great example this past week when you and others publicly expressed your support for me and the program. For this, I will always be appreciative. Actually, I love you for doing so. Sincerely, Barry."

Spring practice arrived in March. Switzer had seemingly held onto his job. He told The Oklahoman's Volney Meece he was looking forward to getting back on the field "moreso than at any time I can remember." But change was

"No jury, no trial, just go hang somebody. Everybody is out to see blood."

— *Former player Anthony Phillips*

in the air. Switzer announced before the start of spring drills he was scrapping his beloved wishbone, in part because the person (Thompson) who would have been running the offense was no longer part of the team.

A week before the start of spring practice, interim university president David Swank made news when speaking to the Texas Daily Newspaper Association in Austin. Swank said the easiest reaction to NCAA probation and the off-the-field incidents of 1989 would have been to fire Switzer.

> "There are changes that will need to be made, but that does not include coach Switzer at this time. ... If he cannot (effect change) then we will have to find someone who can."
>
> — *Interim university president David Swank in 1989*

"There are changes that will need to be made, but that does not include coach Switzer at this time," Swank said, adding that OU's problems were linked to society's tendency to place more emphasis on sports than academics.

Swank expressed confidence that Switzer could effect change. And, Swank added, "If he cannot, then we will have to find someone who can."

Nebraskans – crazy as this sounds – weren't eager to push Switzer out the door. Switzer's record as a head coach against Big Red rival Nebraska was 12-5. But SRI Research Center, Inc., of Lincoln, Neb., conducted a telephone poll of 607 registered voters in March 1989, and 44 percent said Switzer should not resign, according to results published in the Omaha World-Herald. (The rest of the vote, give or take a decimal point: 28 percent said Switzer should resign, 26 percent said they didn't know and 1 percent declined comment.)

Switzer announced his resignation on June 19, 1989. He denied he was under pressure to resign and he urged NCAA reform during a press conference that was carried live by state TV stations. Switzer spent about two hours on the phone with Rick

University of Oklahoma head football coach Barry Switzer resigned on June 19, 1989. The arrest of OU quarterback Charles Thompson for selling cocaine capped a string of negative publicity for the university. The NCAA had placed the school on probation, a player was arrested for shooting a teammate in an athletic dormitory and three other players were accused of sexual assault.

Heisman Trophy winner Steve Owens co-chaired a committee of Switzer loyalists who gathered at an Oklahoma City hotel to show support for the coach in 1989. He is pictured in 1996 when the University of Oklahoma announced his appointment as its athletic director.

Telander that day because he felt the Sports Illustrated writer had treated him fairly in the issue with Thompson on the cover, according to The Tulsa Tribune's Dave Sittler.

Why quit? Switzer said he was physically drained. He didn't divulge details on what caused him to be drained until he wrote "Bootlegger's Boy." Just before resigning, he was summoned to meet with Swank and other OU officials. In the meeting, he was presented with allegations that he had gambled on college football games and manipulated the drug tests of OU players.

"David Swank never fired me and never asked me for my resignation," Switzer told the Tulsa World's Bill Haisten 20 years later. "We never had any conversation in regard to that. All he ever presented to me were accusations and fabrications that were false."

Switzer was zapped by months of defending

himself and his program – and he had wrecked both knees during a skiing trip to Colorado in March 1989. He didn't have the energy to put out another fire.

"They just beat him down to the point where he agreed to step down," former assistant coach Merv Johnson said.

Switzer, asked in 2007 if he regrets not fighting to keep his job, said, "It's not that. I knew their agenda, the hidden agenda. That's why I wrote the book. The only motivation I ever had to write the book was there were a few people with hidden agendas and the lies that were said."

Duncan told Haisten in 2009 that he has never been able to finish Switzer's book and referred to it as a "chronicle of sadness."

Those in Switzer's corner regretted that the curtain closed on his era – and the way it closed.

> "They just beat him down to the point where he agreed to step down."
>
> — *Former assistant coach Merv Johnson*

"I wish he could have left on his own terms instead of being pressured to leave," former player Curtice Williams said. "I hated how the press did him because they tried to make it seem like he was letting us run wild."

Questions were raised as the saga played out:

Was Switzer too lax on discipline?

"If you stepped out of line, he would come down on you hard and sometimes it would be a quiet but painful punishment," Jon Phillips said. "This didn't happen to me, but it happened to one of my roommates, who will remain nameless. He failed a drug test. Well, you had to go sit in Barry Switzer's office and you had to call your mom with him. You had to tell your mother in front of Barry why you failed the drug test and how you were never going to do that to her again. It made an indelible impact. It was far worse than running bleachers until you puked or something like that."

How much responsibility does a coach bear for his players' actions?

Kenny King said players from his era (the 1970s) were allowed to be men and they didn't abuse that. He told Switzer it wasn't his fault that a few individuals went "stupid" in 1989. Said King: "They are grown men. That's their responsibility. But I think a lot of the players, the younger players, they took advantage of him. They took advantage of being allowed to make your own decisions."

> "You had to tell your mother in front of Barry why you failed the drug test and how you were never going to do that to her again. It made an indelible impact. It was far worse than running bleachers until you puked ..."
>
> — *Former player Jon Phillips*

Said Frank Blevins: "He can't watch over us 24/7. There has got to be accountability for each individual there. I don't see how anybody can put the blame on him. I understand that he's the head coach and in the eyes of the public we were out of control. ... You just had some bad apples. I bet if it hadn't happened so close, back to back to back, who knows what the outcome would have been then?"

Was the bootlegger's boy – living proof that you can rise above your past – too willing to give second chances?

"He loved a hard-luck story," Jon Phillips said. "He would love to tell those stories. He loved telling people that (former OU running back) Patrick Collins was one of 16 kids. He loved to tell the story that little Charlie Thompson from Lawton was actually a break dancer at one of our practices. Barry was at some party somewhere back when break dancing was a big deal and this break dancing crew came in and did a routine and he fell so in love with these kids and what they did that he hired them to

WHERE THEY WERE WHEN BARRY SWITZER RESIGNED

Steve Owens

Owens, OU's second Heisman Trophy winner, played for Switzer in 1967-69, when Switzer was an OU assistant.

"I actually was in Norman and at that press conference and had feelings of sadness. Coach Switzer and I came to Oklahoma in the same year when they had the coaching change and I was in the first recruiting class. We were so close and it was a sad day. ... He wasn't going to be the coach at Oklahoma. Coach was special to so many of us. ... It was such a sad day for all of us that loved coach Switzer."

Joe Washington

"Little Joe" was a running back in 1972-75 and helped OU win back-to-back national titles. He is a member of the College Football Hall of Fame.

"I was in Baltimore when I heard it. I was actually home and I think I heard it on the news. I was shocked. Of course, (I was) disappointed because that's my coach. ... The first thing I thought was we're losing an unbelievable resource and folks that allowed him to be let go don't have a clue what they were doing. They have no clue of what they are allowing to happen. ... The next few years, we had decent and fair teams, but we didn't have Switzer years."

Pat Jones

Jones was Oklahoma State's football coach and competed against Switzer and his Sooners in 1984-88.

"My future wife and I were in Maui and we used to go about this time in June every year. We had several days left in our vacation and we had CNN on and she walked by and said something about it. I said something of the effect that we needed to change plans because I needed to get back. They named Gary Gibbs as head coach immediately. We had just moved Johnny Barr up to defensive coordinator and (I knew) Gibbs would try to hire him. We cut our vacation short." (Barr did join OU's staff as linebackers coach.)

Keith Jackson

Jackson is a two-time consensus All-American from Little Rock, Ark., who played tight end for the Sooners in 1984-87.

"I remember being with the Eagles at the time and calling coach on the phone and saying, 'What's up?' He said, 'Keith, you get to the point where you're tired of dealing with all of the issues.' ... He really wants to help kids and do everything he could. ... When he recruited kids, he felt like they were his kids. His frustrations were that the NCAA rules were to the point where it was difficult to just truly take care of the kids the way they should be. I was in Philadelphia when I heard the news. We had a great freshman and redshirt freshman group of guys, a group that went 42-5-1. When we left, a lot of leadership left and a big hole was left."

J.C. Watts

The former wishbone quarterback was 22-3 as a starter (1978-80) and named the most outstanding offensive player in the Orange Bowl during his junior and senior seasons.

"I was a youth pastor at Sunnylane Baptist Church in Del City. That was shocking for all of us that played throughout the decade of the '70s and the '80s. He had established what we did. I just remember being taken aback by it."

come to practice one day and dance for us. Charlie Thompson was one of those dancers. He just loved telling stories about kids getting a chance, especially a hard-luck kid."

Continuing on the topic of Switzer's compassion, Jon Phillips said, "I think I was a junior when (Sooner running back) Anthony Stafford's mother was murdered in St. Louis. I think he found out at practice. They had to pull him off the field at practice and tell him she had been murdered. They were from a rough neighborhood in East St. Louis. Coach handed him his keys and gave him money and said, 'Get on a plane, leave my car at the airport, I don't care. Go. You need to go. Right now.' Of course that was against the rules, but human nature at some point takes over. He's very human. He always would lend a hand to a kid that had no other resource."

Switzer has pointed out that some players made good on second chances. But those kind of stories don't spawn big headlines.

Anthony Phillips said the positive impact Switzer made on young men far outweighs bad things that happened. Over time, others seem to have embraced that too.

"Now the pendulum has swung back and he is universally loved here," Anthony Phillips said. "And, reflecting back on his career and all the people's lives that he has been involved in, I think he has probably got to look back and say, 'It was good.' "

Minus Switzer and set back by NCAA probation, OU posted a .543 winning percentage in the 1990s. That's the worst percent-

> "Now the pendulum has swung back and he is universally loved here. And, reflecting back on his career and all the people's lives that he has been involved in, I think he has probably got to look back and say, 'It was good.' "
>
> — *Former player Anthony Phillips*

Ten years after Barry Switzer's resignation, the University of Oklahoma named its athletic complex in his honor. The Barry Switzer Center was dedicated in 1999. Switzer is shown standing with his family under the new statue of himself, unveiled on the campus in 2011.

Charles Thompson is seen at the Greenwood Cultural Center in Tulsa, where he gave a speech in 2001. After serving his prison time for selling cocaine, Thompson attended college in Ohio and played in the Canadian Football League and the World League. He later became a businessman and motivational speaker.

age of any decade in program history. Switzer has said in multiple interviews that he believes the Sooners would have continued to win at a high level if he had remained the coach because he would have kept homegrown players from leaving the state.

One month before Switzer resigned, he said on his radio show that he would be more tempted than ever to entertain an NFL offer. The phone rang five years later. Jerry Jones was on the other end of the line.

Quarterback Charles Thompson (6) is shown during OU's Nov. 5, 1988, game with Oklahoma State. Thompson's arrest for selling 17 grams of cocaine to an undercover FBI agent put him in prison and was among discipline problems that led to Switzer's resignation.

CHAPTER 10

The book

"This man you would think would be pissed off at the world. But look at his personality."

— Eddie Hinton, on Switzer

After resigning at OU in 1989, Barry Switzer decided to write "Bootlegger's Boy." The experience drew Switzer and his brother Donnie closer together. Donnie confided to Barry that their mother had left a suicide note. Her death wasn't a spontaneous act. Switzer could let go of some guilt.

RECOUNTING HIS PAST

Barry Switzer received a letter in 1988 from a publishing company. Interested in writing a book?

"You have to do something first, don't you?" Switzer told The Tulsa Tribune's Dave Sittler. "Or read one before you write one? I'll get around to that one day. It doesn't interest me now. Hell, with the stuff I'd have to leave out, it wouldn't be much of a book."

Switzer quickly found time to write "Bootlegger's Boy" after parting company with OU. He was right about leaving out a lot of things (1,500 pages worth of material had to be edited down to 406 pages). He was wrong that it wouldn't be much of a book. It was a bestseller that detailed stunning moments for readers.

Switzer pulled back the curtain on what led to his departure from OU and shared deeply personal stories about his mother's suicide and what it was like to be the child of a bootlegger.

Former player Eddie Hinton read the book. All of a sudden, his relationship with Switzer made a lot more sense.

An introduction to Hinton: Prentice Gautt broke OU's color barrier when he joined the football team in 1956. A decade later, Hinton was among the Sooners' first great African-American players. He was an All-Big Eight wingback in 1968 and he was a first-round pick of the Baltimore Colts in 1969. He caught two passes for 51 yards in a 16-13 victory over the Dallas Cowboys in Super Bowl V.

Hinton was a sophomore when new coach Jim Mackenzie brought a fresh crop of assistant coaches to Norman in 1966. One of the new assistants was Switzer, who seemed determined to befriend Hinton.

"And I wasn't used to a coach getting close to me," Hinton said. "I think his wife at the time was Kay. We would go to a

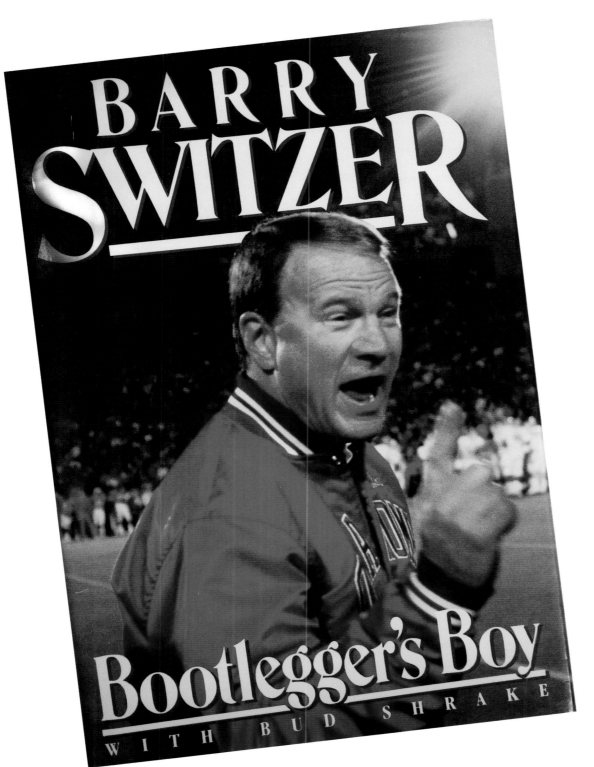

Barry Switzer's memoir, "Bootlegger's Boy," was published in 1990. In it, he told what led to his departure from OU and shared deeply personal stories about his family.

Eddie Hinton, who played at OU from 1966-68, said he found out when he read Barry Switzer's book that he and the coach had something in common: parents who were bootleggers.

game or something and they would always want to sit next to me. He always would say, 'I just love you, Eddie.' And I'm like, 'Hey man, what's wrong with you? Are you gay or something?' I didn't know how to take it because I never had any man – because my mother raised us – that was interested in me."

It took years for Hinton to realize Switzer just cared, period. Maybe the bootlegger's boy saw something of himself in Hinton, who said he came from a family of bootleggers in Lawton, Okla.

"That's basically why I got into sports and played in the band is because I really didn't want to go home because we ran our business right out of the house," Hinton said. "I'm sure Barry knew all that. He kind of found out about that."

Hinton discovered how much he and Switzer had in common when he read the coach's book.

"He couldn't date the nice white girls," Hinton said. " ... and I couldn't date the nice black girls because my parents were bootleggers and I was sort of classified as the bad guy. You would go to church and your mother would make you go and we always had nice clothes and we had go-carts and motorcycles and we would have birthday parties and we would invite the

> "He couldn't date the nice white girls ... and I couldn't date the nice black girls because my parents were bootleggers and I was sort of classified as the bad guy."
>
> — *Eddie Hinton, former OU player*

neighborhood, but they never invited us to theirs.

"So I played all sports – football, basketball, ran track, baseball, anything to stay busy to find some kind of positives that I'm a nice guy."

Initial attempts by Switzer to dig into Hinton's background were blocked. Said Hinton: "What do you want, man? Why do you keep asking me stuff?"

They had only one major run-in, according to Hinton. The problem? Hinton was deceptively smooth in his practice work and had a burning desire to never let a coach see him fatigued.

"Eddie was such an athlete that when he ran, it was like a gazelle running," former teammate Mike Harper said. "There wasn't any effort to it at all. The rest of us were struggling to run and he was gliding along and Switzer always thought he was loafing, but he wasn't."

Switzer ordered Hinton to do some extra running after a workout. Hinton did more extra running

Eddie Hinton, a Sooner running back in the 1960s, was deceptively smooth in practice and never wanted to let a coach see him fatigued, according to an Oklahoma teammate.

OU's Eddie Hinton catches the ball during a game. Hinton, of Lawton, Okla., was a first-round draft pick of the Baltimore Colts after his college career. The wide receiver caught two passes in a 16-13 victory over the Dallas Cowboys in Super Bowl V.

than he was asked to do and gave Switzer a "look" every time he passed the coach.

Hinton looks back now and realizes Switzer was just trying to squeeze the best out of him. Another of those occasions came before a game against Missouri.

Switzer put his arm on Hinton's shoulder at the stadium.

Switzer: "You know we're playing Missouri today, Ed?"

Hinton: "Coach, we've been watching film and getting prepared for them all week."

Switzer: "Yeah, but do you know they have an All-American defensive back, No. 22, named Roger Wehrli?"

Hinton: "Yeah coach, I'm aware of him."

Switzer: "He's going to kick your ass today."

Hinton was shocked.

But Switzer wasn't finished. Added the coach, "Guess what Hinton? He's white, too."

The intent was to push Hinton's buttons. It worked.

"And I wasn't used to a coach getting close to me. I think his wife at the time was Kay. We would go to a game ... and they would always want to sit next to me. He always would say, 'I just love you, Eddie.' And I'm like 'Hey man, what's wrong with you? Are you gay or something?' "

— *Eddie Hinton, former OU player*

"They kicked off to us," Hinton said. "I ran back the kickoffs and the punts. And all I can think of is I've got that No. 22 in my brain. He is on defense on the kickoff. And it felt like the whole field opened up. I didn't care about anybody else. I see this No. 22. And I've got the ball and I'm running toward him hollering his name. I could have gone right or left, but Barry had me so psyched up that every time I saw him on the field, I said 'Roger, I'm coming!' "

Switzer's bromance with Hinton continued beyond their time together on campus. Switzer once had tickets for a big boxing match in Las Vegas and he pestered Hinton until he agreed to attend the fight. Celebrities such as Sylvester Stallone were coming out of the woodwork for a pre-fight party. And in walks Muhammad Ali with an entourage. Switzer told a funny story about his encounter with Ali in "Bootlegger's Boy."

Switzer's partner in writing the book was Edwin "Bud" Shrake, a journalist, novelist and screenwriter whose life was as epic as Switzer's.

Switzer sat down with Shrake for about two weeks to spill his guts for what would become "Bootlegger's Boy." One of the good things to come out of the experience was Switzer and his younger brother Donnie grew closer while piecing together a shared past. Donnie confided to Barry for the first time that he had found a suicide note from their mother. Her death wasn't a spontaneous act. Barry could let go of some guilt.

> ## "Eddie was such an athlete that when he ran, it was like a gazelle running."
>
> — *Mike Harper, on his OU teammate Eddie Hinton*

"I still wonder how he and his brother were able to come through all that," Hinton said.

"This man you would think would be pissed off at the world. But look at his personality."

Hinton eventually succumbed to the coach with the big personality.

"With his consistency of him being who he is, I finally appreciated him," Hinton said. "I know I missed out a lot probably getting to really know him. But it's OK. I'm knowing him now."

Barry Switzer signs copies of "Bootlegger's Boy" and other Sooner memorabilia in Tulsa in 1998.

CHAPTER 11

Dallas Cowboys

"Jerry (Jones) just calls and says, 'Do you want the job?' I said, 'If the job is open, I'd be interested.' He says, 'The job is going to be open. I'm going to fire Jimmy tomorrow. Get in the car and drive down here.' I got in the car and drove to Dallas."

— Barry Switzer

When Barry Switzer accepted the coaching job with the Dallas Cowboys in 1994, he rejoined his longtime friend, Larry Lacewell, who had been hired by the team as director of scouting. "I wouldn't be here if it wasn't for Larry," Switzer told Sports Illustrated.

CHASING THE LOMBARDI TROPHY

Larry Lacewell and Barry Switzer were naked in the swimming pool. It's not what you think.

Lacewell grew up in Fordyce, Ark., about 70 miles from Switzer's hometown of Crossett, Ark. They first met as 10th graders because they were competing in a state swimming and diving meet.

"They would put us in the YMCA and, back in those days, for cleanliness purposes, we couldn't wear bathing suits," Lacewell said. "We swam naked in the YMCA."

Lacewell, smiling, couldn't resist adding this: "I think Switzer noticed me then."

Continued Lacewell, "Anyhow, we played poker and we didn't know how to play poker. My buddy from Fordyce and I, we weren't smart enough to stay out of poker games with Barry and a guy named Billy Ray Greenwood. They won all our money. We had to hitchhike to Fordyce and they rode the bus by us and honked. That's my first memory of Barry."

Lacewell and the kid who cleaned him out at the poker table became friends. They never played high school football against each other, but they sort of shared a field during Lacewell's senior season.

"I made one of those Joe Washington runs," Lacewell said. "The problem was I went backwards and couldn't come forward. It was the first play of the game. I broke out of the pack and ran to the boundary after what was going to be about a 20-yard loss. And I got hit by about 13 guys – it took that many to get me on the ground – and sure enough it knocks me right into the crowd. People in little towns like that would crowd the sideline. I looked up and I hear this voice say, 'Great run, Lacewell.' It was Switzer. He and his buddies had come to the game on Thursday night to watch us play."

Like boomerangs, Barry Layne and Larry Wayne kept landing in the same spot.

When he joined the Dallas Cowboys, Barry Switzer was reunited with quarterback Troy Aikman, who had been a starter for the Sooners in 1985 until suffering a broken ankle in his fourth outing. He later transferred to UCLA. Aikman, who graduated from high school in Henryetta, Okla., is shown during a game against the Green Bay Packers in 1996.

When Switzer was an Arkansas senior, Lacewell was an Alabama graduate assistant under Fordyce's favorite son, Bear Bryant. Lacewell wanted to catch up with college pals, so he spent a couple of nights at Switzer's house outside of Crossett.

Switzer and Lacewell were staffmates under Jim Mackenzie at Oklahoma in 1966. Lacewell left and came back, eventually becoming Switzer's defensive coordinator. Lacewell bolted after the 1977 season because their relationship went south. But if you saw them holding court at the 2014 Kentucky Derby, you know goodbye didn't last forever.

In between was another shared gig.

Lacewell was hired by the Dallas Cowboys in 1992 as director of scouting. Cowboys owner Jerry Jones and head coach Jimmy Johnson parted ways after the 1993 season, despite that the tandem had won back-to-back Super Bowls. Jones needed a coach. He called Switzer, who had been an assistant coach at Arkansas when Jones and Johnson were Razorback linemen.

> "Jerry Jones loved Switzer. ... He really wanted a guy – I don't want to use the word 'caretaker' – but he didn't want to bring some big shot in there with an ego who would bust up our team."
>
> — *Larry Lacewell*

Switzer, after taking the job, told Sports Illustrated, "I wouldn't be here if it wasn't for Larry."

True? "Jerry Jones loved Switzer," Lacewell said. "When Jerry was in the oil business in Oklahoma City, he was down in our offices a lot and he knew Barry. He really wanted a guy – I don't want to use the word 'caretaker' – but he didn't want to bring some big shot in there with an ego who would bust up our team. We knew what we were. We knew we had a great team.

"Anyway, I think Jerry had in the back of his mind who he wanted. I think Jerry started making his plans. As a matter of fact, I think they hired Barry just thinking that I was all for it. But I was never against it. I thought he was perfect for what we

Barry Switzer (left) and Cowboys owner Jerry Jones walk to a news conference where Jones announced Switzer as the new coach of the Dallas Cowboys on March 30, 1994.

Switzer took over a well-established Cowboys team in 1994. "I was there to keep this thing in the middle of the road. Same playbook. Same offense. Same defense. Why change it? Why change the staff? They had won two Super Bowls," Switzer said.

were looking for."

Switzer told the Tulsa World's Bill Haisten in 2009 that there was no interview process. "Jerry just calls and says, 'Do you want the job?' I said, 'If the job is open, I'd be interested.' He says, 'The job is going to be open. I'm going to fire Jimmy tomorrow. Get in the car and drive down here.' I got in the car and drove to Dallas."

Donnie Duncan, who had been Switzer's last athletic director at Oklahoma, and 1969 Heisman Trophy winner Steve Owens were among those present at an introductory press conference.

"We have a job to do and we're going to do it, baby!" Switzer said.

Not everyone was as enthusiastic. Star receiver Michael Irvin chucked a trash can at TV cameras upon learning that Switzer was replacing the man who had coached him in college. Irvin walked out of the first team meeting with Switzer. Meanwhile, offensive tackle Mark Tuinei told the Dallas Morning News it was hard to believe Switzer coached Jones and Johnson at Arkansas.

"He looks younger than they do," Tuinei said. "But he'll age quickly here."

> " … I just told him we still had a good football team and come on back and he did. And, hey, let me tell you something, a couple of million dollars will make you come back pretty fast. Let's be honest."
>
> — *Larry Lacewell*

Recalled Switzer in 2009: "I had a tough job. Think about it. I didn't get to hire any coaches. I've got to go in there and take over a bunch of guys, and I don't know their hidden agendas or what their loyalty would be. I was there to keep this thing in the middle of the road. Same playbook. Same offense. Same defense. Why change it? Why change the staff? They had won two Super Bowls."

The contrast between Switzer (he was the opposite of a micromanager) and Johnson was stark.

Said Lacewell, "Jimmy loved to play the role of 'I'm the head coach and you're not.' And Barry was just the opposite. We all were coaches. And that was his personality. ... People didn't quite understand that Barry didn't want to be the general."

Lacewell said "enemies" fed things to players about Switzer, and some of it was probably the truth. For instance, Switzer didn't burn the candle at both ends in the football offices.

"He was older," Lacewell said. "He had been out of coaching five years. He did it his way and, in the beginning, it wasn't very good. The players didn't adapt to it. But, eventually, the Michael Irvins and the Deion Sanders and the Emmitt Smiths, they loved him."

The Cowboys were quarterbacked by Troy Aikman, who started his college career at OU under Switzer and transferred to UCLA. They began the Switzer era 11-2, but the expectation was a Lombardi Trophy. His first season ended with a 38-28 loss to the rival San Francisco 49ers in the NFC championship game.

> "He had been out of coaching five years. He did it his way and, in the beginning, it wasn't very good. The players didn't adapt to it. But, eventually, the Michael Irvins and the Deion Sanders and the Emmitt Smiths, they loved him."
>
> —*Larry Lacewell*

Switzer was asked by the Tulsa World in 2007 if he would like to have a do-over of any games in his career. He mentioned the 1978 OU-Nebraska game (the Sooners fumbled nine times, losing six, and fell out of the national championship chase) and his first NFC title game. He said the Cowboys self-destructed.

"Crap, we ain't snapped the ball twice and we're down 21-0. That doesn't make sense," Switzer said, referring to a game in which the 49ers converted three turnovers into touchdowns in the first eight minutes.

Dallas Cowboys (from left) Michael Irvin, Troy Aikman and Emmitt Smith celebrate during the Super Bowl in 1996. The Cowboys defeated the Steelers, 27-17.

"That really disappointed me because whoever wins that game wins the Super Bowl. Whoever goes and plays San Diego in the Super Bowl is going to win it. (The Cowboys) would have won four in a row and I would have won two in a row."

The Cowboys settled for three championships in four years by winning Super Bowl XXX the following season. During a postgame celebration, Irvin threw praise instead of a trash can. Sports Illustrated reported that Irvin shouted this to partiers:

"Is there anyone who deserves this more than Barry Switzer?"

Switzer told the Tulsa World's Bill Haisten in 2009 that he should have resigned after winning the Super Bowl. Lacewell talked him out of it.

> "Crap, we ain't snapped the ball twice and we're down 21-0. That doesn't make sense. That really disappointed me because whoever wins that game wins the Super Bowl."
>
> —*Barry Switzer*

"I think I did," Lacewell said. "I said, 'Barry, this isn't the time to quit.' I said, 'You will always wonder.' He probably should have quit frankly. But I didn't want him to. I was selfish. I'm worried about my own future. I had known Jimmy. I had known Barry. So who the hell am I going to work for the next year? I just told him we still had a good football team and come on back and he did. And, hey, let me tell you something, a couple of million dollars will make you come back pretty fast. Let's be honest."

Switzer stuck around for two more seasons and resigned after a 6-10 campaign in 1997. The Cowboys have won one playoff game since. Lacewell contends Switzer was hamstrung by the implementation of the salary cap in 1994.

"Jimmy never had to coach under the cap at that time," Lacewell said. "We started losing players and we couldn't afford to keep them. We were a great team. We couldn't afford to keep them all. You could see the slide down. It wasn't Switzer's fault. But at the same time, Switzer was not going to put in 24 hours a day. His career was behind him, you understand."

Switzer has said he couldn't care less what critics say about his time as an NFL coach. What should people think about his tour of duty with the Dallas Cowboys?

Said Lacewell, "He did what he needed to do. He didn't screw up a good football team. He was a caretaker in the right sense. The offensive staff liked him. The defensive staff liked him. Players eventually really liked him. To win national championships and a Super Bowl is a pretty good career. People said he did it with Jimmy's players, but you are always going to do it with somebody's players. He didn't screw it up, by any means."

Lacewell said they had a good time in Dallas. Good times continue. About that Kentucky Derby trip in 2014 ...

The night before the race, Lacewell said he and Switzer were at a "big shot" hotel and it was packed with people. Lacewell caroused until

Barry Switzer holds the Super Bowl XXX trophy on Jan. 28, 1996. With the win, Dallas became the first team to win three Super Bowls in four years.

After a disappointing 6-10 season in 1997, Switzer resigned as head coach of the Dallas Cowboys with a 40-24 career NFL coaching record.

around midnight and decided enough was enough. He headed for his room. Switzer started walking through the hotel and people began hollering at him. He stayed and talked football until the wee hours.

"If Barry was a butthole, I wouldn't want to be around him," Lacewell said. "Jerry Jones doesn't treat people badly. I don't think I do. But Barry is extremely nice to people so it makes it an enjoyable trip. He doesn't get mad about a plane being late and he doesn't get upset. I remember (a Cowboys team) plane was delayed in Mexico when we played down there. We couldn't get off the ground for two hours. We were all saying if Jimmy had been there, he would have thrown a fit and called the president and everything. Switzer just sat back on the plane and laughed and cut up and talked to the players."

Opposite: Barry Switzer gets doused after winning Super Bowl XXX at Sun Devil Stadium in Tempe, Ariz., in 1996. The Cowboys defeated the Pittsburgh Steelers, 27–17.

CHAPTER 12

'I've got you, big boy'

"I would bet my life that there are many, many, many players he has helped. He's just a humble guy and he is not going to talk about it because we are his kids."

— *Louis Oubre, on Barry Switzer*

Barry Switzer organized a fundraising campaign after hearing that his former player, Louis Oubre, had lost everything in the devastation of Hurricane Katrina in 2005. Switzer and his wife, Becky, escorted a moving truck full of furniture and other household goods to Oubre's family in Houston.

GOING THE EXTRA MILE

Barry Switzer left the Dallas Cowboys in 1997.

Former OU and NFL offensive lineman Louis Oubre left New Orleans eight years later. Oubre's plan was to settle in his hometown and coach high school blockers. Hurricane Katrina proved unblockable.

Oubre and his fiancée Dana (she's his wife now) beat the storm out of town as part of a mass exodus. More than 200,000 people left for higher ground. Oubre drove to Texas before finding a hotel with a vacancy.

The levees protecting New Orleans failed. Approximately 80 percent of the town was under floodwaters. The death toll was nearly 1,000. Maybe Oubre was lucky that the only thing he lost was everything.

"All my wife walked out with was her purse," he said. "I had an extra pair of gym shorts because they were in the back of my truck already."

Oubre spent three weeks in the hotel and, with nothing to return to in New Orleans, he filed paperwork for housing assistance so he could remain in the Dallas area.

"I got an apartment, a three-bedroom, because my wife had two kids," he said. "It was a nice big apartment, but we didn't have any furniture. We were sleeping on the floor, on mattresses on the floor."

Oubre phoned his college coach and told him about the predicament.

"I need your help," Oubre said.

Switzer's response: "I've got you, big boy."

Oubre said he called Switzer on a Wednesday or Thursday. Switzer staged an amateur telethon for help, chipping in $1,000

Louis Oubre was an offensive lineman at the University of Oklahoma from 1976 through 1980.
He was a National Merit Scholarship contender at St. Augustine High School in New Orleans.

and raising close to $10,000. On Saturday, a moving truck full of furniture arrived at Oubre's residence. The truck had an escort: Switzer and his second wife, Becky, tagged along in another vehicle to oversee delivery.

"I'm thinking he's just coming maybe to drop off a couple of things," Oubre said. "Man, he came with a king-sized bed, two twin beds for my kids and he's got mattresses and box springs. One, two, three TVs. A dining room set. A living room set. A sofa. Another big TV. Lamps. Pots. Pans. Clothes for the kids. You name it, he came up with it."

Katrina blew Oubre out of New Orleans. Switzer's generosity blew him away.

Wind the clock back to Oubre's recruitment in the 1970s: Oubre was a National Merit Scholarship contender while attending St. Augustine High School in New Orleans. He could have gotten his education paid for without putting on shoulder pads. He received over 100 academic scholarship offers, some from institutions with ivy on the walls. Switzer out-recruited the brainy schools and the football factories. Or, as Oubre put it, "He charmed my mama's socks off."

When Alabama's Bear Bryant called late at night, Oubre's mother said this: "I don't care who this is. My son is going to sleep and we are not going to wake him up."

Oubre's parents were happy to take Switzer's calls and they treated the coach to red beans every time he came to visit. Oubre said his mother was a pretty good judge of character. She believed Switzer when he promised to take care of her son. After Katrina, Switzer was still keeping his vow.

"All the money in the world couldn't repay what he has done for me," Oubre said, suggesting that Switzer transformed him and many other players from boys to men. "And, talking about Hurricane Katrina, I was down and out. Broke. I had to cash in some other investments so we could stay in a hotel. Coach turned it all around. And then he pointed out what had happened to me and other people started sending us money so we had a little nest egg to kind of get us back on our feet where we could buy

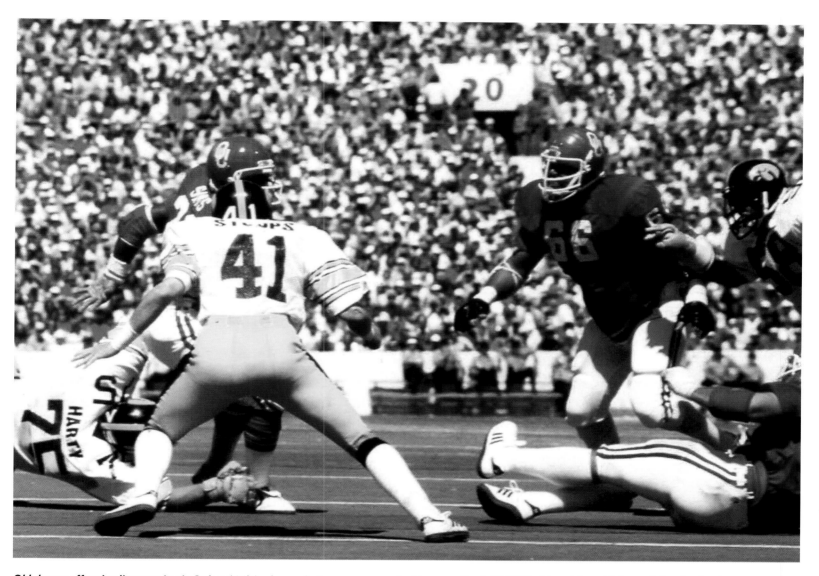

Oklahoma offensive lineman Louis Oubre (66) is shown during a game against Iowa on Sept. 15, 1979. Also pictured is Iowa defensive back Bob Stoops (41), the future head coach of the Sooners, who is trying to tackle Billy Sims. OU won the game, 21-6.

a house. He kind of saved us."

Oubre knows he's not the only former Sooner rescued by Switzer. "I'm sure he has done that for player after player after player. That's how he is. He takes care of you. If he recruits you, you are his for life."

Oubre needed Switzer again in 2011.

Oubre's former roommate, two-time All-America guard Terry Crouch, died in May of that year. He was 51.

"He didn't have insurance, so his wife didn't have enough money to bury him," Oubre said. "So I started a little fund to help with the burial and maybe put a little money in the wife's pocket. We had raised like maybe $3,000."

Oubre phoned Switzer, who said he would make a few calls.

"By the time he finished, I had $7,500," Oubre said. "He gave about a thousand and then he made some calls and then some other people started sending like $500 checks."

Oubre needed Switzer on one more occasion.

After putting down roots in Texas, Oubre and Dana decided to get married. Oubre asked Switzer and other former OU coaches to be in the wedding.

"Man, he came with a king-sized bed, two twin beds for my kids and he's got mattresses and box springs. One, two, three TVs. A dining room set. A living room set. A sofa. Another big TV. Lamps. Pots. Pans. Clothes for the kids. You name it, he came up with it."

—Louis Oubre, *former OU player*

Opposite: Former OU head coach Barry Switzer introduces former players prior to the Red/White Scrimmage.

Oubre arranged for a band to play at the wedding reception. He told the band he wanted to sing "My Girl" to his bride. And he did, with some help.

"Coach Switzer jumped up onstage and he was up there singing," Oubre said. "It was a great time."

The men in Oubre's wedding party were asked to wear white tuxedos with pink accessories.

"Oh no," Switzer said. "You better not tell anybody about this."

Almost immediately, Oubre posted Facebook photos of Switzer wearing pink and white. Switzer had plenty of reasons to forgive Oubre, a 1980 All-American who opened holes for Heisman Trophy winner Billy Sims while in Norman.

Sims, referring to Switzer's actions following Hurricane Katrina, said, "Coach Switzer has done an 'Oubre' 100 times that I know of, helping people that the media doesn't even know about."

> "Coach Switzer jumped up onstage and he was up there singing. It was a great time."
>
> —*Louis Oubre, about his wedding reception*

Said Oubre: "I would bet my life that there are many, many, many players he has helped. He's just a humble guy and he is not going to talk about it because we are his kids. I'm sure he has helped Billy Sims over the years. Coach is a giving guy. He's not one of those guys that once you play for him, you are forgotten. When he says he loves you, he actually loves you. There is no fake in it."

Opposite: Louis Oubre (66) protects Oklahoma quarterback J.C. Watts (1) during a game against the University of Tulsa in 1979. Barry Switzer raised money for Oubre after Oubre's family lost everything to Hurricane Katrina in 2005.

Barry Switzer wore a white tuxedo with pink accessories to Louis Oubre's wedding.

Oubre is a coach in Cedar Hill, Texas. If he owes anything to Switzer, he's paying it forward. Oubre posted this about himself on a school website:

"I am a teacher because of my love of children, and my need to fill a void in the educational system. This void is caused by a lack of effective teachers and a shortage of positive male role models. I have been abundantly blessed throughout my life. It is time that I give back to society what society has given to me. I have done numerous things which have afforded me experiences and opportunities of which others only dream. I have made many mistakes in my life; However, these mistakes have been valuable learning experiences. I can now use these mistakes as a learning tool for our children. I need to make a difference!"

Opposite: The Barry Switzer Center opened in Norman, Okla., in 1999. The University of Oklahoma complex houses the locker room, support areas, strength and training areas, coaches' offices and the Legends Lobby.

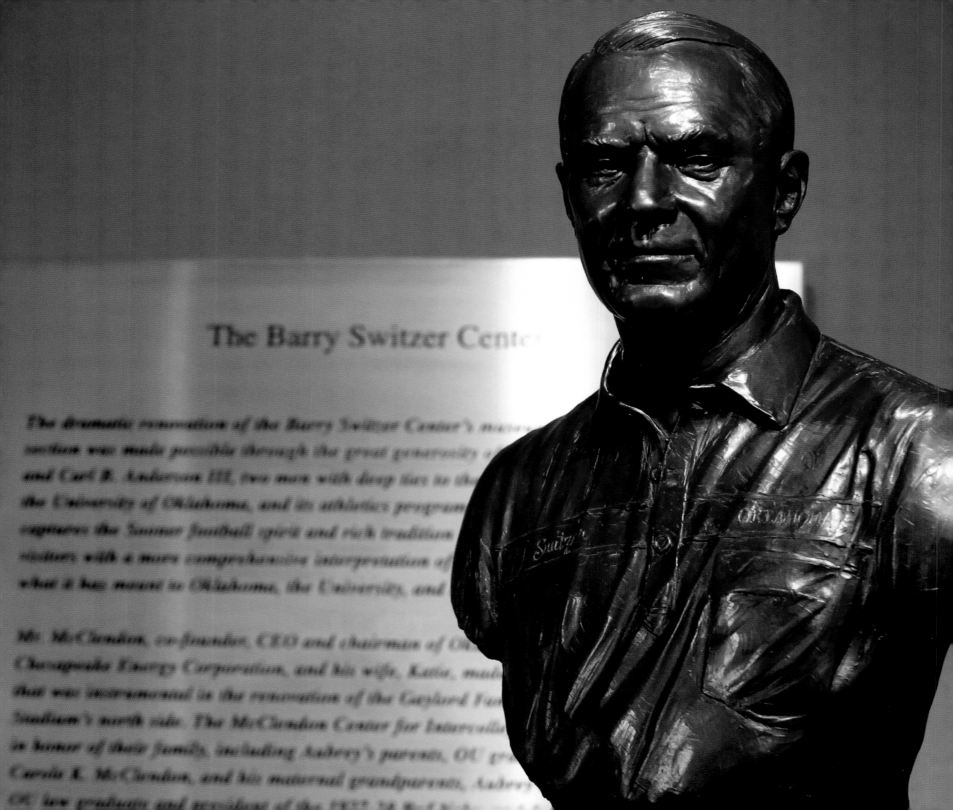

CHAPTER 13

Playing overtime

"I'm going to say there might be 1,000 kids that played for Barry Switzer and everybody feels like they are his best friend ... "

— *Grant Burget*

A bust of Barry Switzer is among the items displayed inside the Barry Switzer Center on the University of Oklahoma campus in Norman, Okla.

WHAT BEST FRIENDS ARE FOR

Grant Burget attended Super Bowl XXX and enjoyed watching his former coach become a champion again. He was invited to Barry Switzer's hotel suite and watched Dallas Cowboy players trickle in for a postgame party he'll never forget.

It was the highlight of Switzer's professional career. A lowlight for Burget came soon afterward. Burget got this news from a doctor: "You've got two years to live."

Burget is a former Oklahoma halfback from Stroud, Okla. He's the reason Switzer's mood was tempered after his head coaching debut in 1973. OU roared to a 35-0 halftime lead in a 42-14 smashing of Baylor. Switzer should have been all smiles, but expressed regret that Burget wrecked a knee.

Burget missed the remainder of that season and returned to play on an unbeaten national championship squad as a senior in 1974.

Burget launched a more significant comeback in the late 1990s, this time from throat cancer.

When a tumor was discovered near the base of Burget's tongue, a doctor warned Burget he was living on borrowed time.

The fight for survival began with a surgical procedure that lasted more than 13 hours.

Opposite: Grant Burget was a running back on Barry Switzer's first Sooner team as head coach. Since then, he has survived throat cancer, a heart attack and a stroke. Through it all, he said, his former coach was by his side.

"I thought the surgery was going to be bad," Burget said. "But then I had to go through a radiation treatment and I said, 'This will be a breeze.' And the doctor said, 'Oh no, man, it's going to be worse than the surgery.' I had to do five days a week for six weeks, 30 treatments."

Burget said he was ready to quit after treatment No. 24 or 25.

"I'm not coming back," he said.

> "I thought the surgery was going to be bad. But then I had to go through a radiation treatment and I said, 'This will be a breeze.' And the doctor said, 'Oh no, man, it's going to be worse than the surgery.' "
>
> — *Grant Burget*

A doctor urged Burget to take a few days off. Burget took the advice, got his second wind, completed the treatments and has lived far beyond the initial projection.

Burget recalled his battle with cancer during an interview in 2014. He turned emotional and his voice cracked when he recalled this part of the story: Switzer was still the head coach of the Dallas Cowboys when news of the tumor was delivered. An NFL season was in full swing, but Switzer hopped on a Jerry Jones jet and flew to Oklahoma City to surprise Burget in the hospital.

In better times, it was Switzer who had provided Burget with a Super Bowl ticket. It wasn't the first time the coach did Burget a favor at a bowl.

Switzer coached in the Hula Bowl, a college all-star game, after his second season at the OU helm. Burget and some pals were in Hawaii during the Hula Bowl because they had flown there to relax. When USC running back Anthony Davis was scratched from the Hula Bowl roster because of an injury, Switzer approached Burget: "You want to play?"

OU quarterback Steve Davis (5) hands the ball off to Grant Burget (25) during the OU-Baylor game in 1974. A year earlier, Burget had wrecked his knee during the Baylor game.

One of Oklahoma's seven national championship trophies is shown in the Barry Switzer Center at OU.

Barry Switzer coached in the Hula Bowl, the college all-star game, in Hawaii after his second season as OU's head coach. Switzer invited Grant Burget, who was vacationing in Hawaii, to join the team after USC's Anthony Davis was scratched due to injury. "Only Switzer would think of something like that," Burget said.

Said Burget, "I actually had to go to a high school there locally and get some pads and I practiced two days and played in the Hula Bowl. That was fun. Only Switzer would think of something like that."

In years following the cancer scare, Burget suffered a heart attack and a stroke. More recently, he was stricken by what he described as two "mini-strokes." Again, Switzer was an encourager. "And he still is," Burget said.

Burget suspects he knows Switzer better than many former players because he and the coach spent many Saturdays together. One of Burget's college roommates was Gary Gibbs, who became Switzer's defensive coordinator and successor. That led to Burget helping out the coaching staff on game days. He lent a hand in the press box and traveled to road games.

While acknowledging his bond with Switzer is special, Burget also said this: "I'm going to say there might be 1,000 kids that played for Barry Switzer and everybody feels like they are his best friend – and not only former players, but coaches and people he runs across in business and people he has had relationships with over a long period of time. They just all think he is one of their best friends."

That's winning.

ACKNOWLEDGMENTS

Thanks are owed to the many former University of Oklahoma players who were interviewed for this book. Thanks also go to Shelby Bryan (alias Mrs. Tater Hill), former Arkansas player Jim Mooty and former OU assistant coaches Larry Lacewell, Merv Johnson and Bill Michael.

Among people responsible for providing contacts or pointing the author in the right direction are former Oklahoma State coach Pat Jones, KJRH sports director/Tulsa Sports Animal radio host Al Jerkens, Hawgs Illustrated publisher Clay Henry, sports memorabilia expert Robert Taylor and Tommy Thompson, whose annual Heisman golf tournament in Tulsa is populated by players who are quoted prominently in this book.

Barry Switzer's longtime buddy, Billy Joe Holder, provided a guided tour of Crossett, Ark., for the author and photographer Michael Wyke. Thanks to everyone in Crossett who played a role in making the book possible.

Many outstanding writers at the state's major newspapers did a great job of chronicling the Switzer era. Their entertaining stories made research feel like the opposite of work.

Thanks to the University of Oklahoma and the University of Arkansas for their cooperation.

Thanks to Tulsa World teammates, including Debbie Jackson, Matt Lardner, Christopher Smith and Hilary Pittman, for making the book far better than it would have been without their assistance. Tulsa World designers (Tim Chamberlin, James Royal and Jason Powers) and photographers provided the book with a "wow" factor. And thanks to the folks at the Tulsa World for trusting the author with the project.

Of course, thanks are owed to the subject of this book, Barry Switzer. He's a busy person, even in retirement, and his time is appreciated.

ABOUT THE AUTHOR

Jimmie Tramel was chosen the Oklahoma Sports Writer of the Year in 2013 by the National Sportscasters and Sportswriters Association. Raised in Locust Grove, Okla., Tramel has been a writer at the Tulsa World since 1989 and he wrote a book with former Oklahoma State coach Pat Jones in 2007. Tramel lives in the Tulsa area with his wife, Vicki, and their children, Katie and Kal.

APPENDIX

Barry Switzer — Career head coaching statistics

College
University of Oklahoma (1973-1988), 157-29-4 (.837), 3 national championships, 12 Big Eight conference titles

Season	Overall	Big 8	Bowl	Highlights
1973	10-0-1	7-0	None due to NCAA probation	Big Eight Championship
1974	11-0	7-0	None due to NCAA probation	National Championship, Big Eight Championship
1975	11-1	6-1	Orange Bowl, W, 14-6 vs. Michigan	National Championship, Big Eight Championship
1976	9-2-1	5-2	Fiesta Bowl, W, 41-7 vs. Wyoming	Big Eight Championship
1977	10-2	7-0	Orange Bowl, L, 31-6 vs. Arkansas	Big Eight Championship
1978	11-1	6-1	Orange Bowl, W, 31-24 vs. Nebraska	Billy Sims wins Heisman Trophy, Big Eight Championship
1979	11-1	7-0	Orange Bowl, W, 24-7 vs. Florida State	Big Eight Championship
1980	10-2	7-0	Orange Bowl, W, 18-17 vs. Florida State	Big Eight Championship
1981	7-4-1	4-2-1	Sun Bowl, W, 40-14 vs. Houston	
1982	8-4	6-1	Fiesta Bowl, L, 32-21 vs. Arizona State	
1983	8-4	5-2	None	
1984	9-2-1	6-1	Orange Bowl, L, 28-17 vs. Washington	Big Eight Championship
1985	11-1	7-0	Orange Bowl, W, 25-10 vs. Penn State	National Championship, Big Eight Championship
1986	11-1	7-0	Orange Bowl, W, 42-8 vs. Arkansas	Big Eight Championship
1987	11-1	7-0	Orange Bowl, L, 20-14 vs. Miami	Big Eight Championship
1988	9-3	6-1	Citrus Bowl, L, 13-6 vs. Clemson	

NFL
Dallas Cowboys (1994-1997), 40-24-0* (.625), 1995 Super Bowl championship, 1 NFC championship,
3 NFC East division championships

Season	Record	Playoffs	Highlights
1994	12-4	1-1	NFC East Championship
1995	12-4	3-0	NFC East Championship, NFC Championship, Super Bowl Championship
1996	10-6	1-1	NFC East Championship
1997	6-10	None	

*Does not include playoffs | Sources: www.soonersports.com, www.pro-football-reference.com

PHOTOGRAPHERS CREDITS

INDEX